SHROPSHIRE'S CENTURY SPEAKS

Edited by Genevieve Tudor

Interviews by Chris Eldon Lee

Shropshire
Books

ISBN: 0-903802-77-5
Text © BBC
Cover and book design: The Graphic Terrace
Managing Editor: Helen Sample
Published by Shropshire Books, the publishing imprint of Shropshire
County Council's Community and Environment Department.
Printed in Great Britain by PCP, Telford.

CONTENTS

ACKNOWLEDGEMENTS

My grateful thanks to the people of Shropshire for their kindness, interest and trust.

Thanks to the BBC, particularly to BBC Radio Shropshire, who kindly allowed me free rein at the station and to Chris Eldon Lee who interviewed the people of Shropshire for this project.

The photographs in the book were kindly loaned by the contributors, taken on site by Genevieve Tudor, or reproduced courtesy of Shropshire Records and Research Unit.

Genevieve Tudor
Editor

FOREWORD

It is the depth and breadth of The Century Speaks that impresses me most.

100 voices. 100 years. 1000s of memories. With this book and the sixteen BBC Radio Shropshire programmes, you too will be able to take rare glimpses into the lives, loves, beliefs and fears of a century of Salopians.

My oldest interviewee was Maisie of Whitchurch who at 103 could remember being given a grey velvet dress to wear on the day of Queen Victoria's funeral.

The youngest was 12 year old Darren from Bridgnorth who remembered Dwight Yorke's last goal for Aston Villa. Solemn occasions both.

I met Maisie and Darren in the same week at the start of 1999. I had asked for a two hour interview and both made an effort to fit me into their busy schedules.

Maisie went to India at the age of twenty in 1916 to do a little hospital work and there met and married a Methodist minister. The only private place for courtship was on the flat roof of a nearby house. On her wedding night servants lay sweet-smelling cut Eucalyptus branches under her bed and fed her on curried goat. In India Maisie rode a camel. Back in Britain she had one of the first cars in the area - a Sunbeam Tourer which her father and his coachman both learnt to drive side by side. Maisie herself only gave up driving her car at the age of 95. Five years later, on her hundredth birthday she still only felt about fifty and she hopes to stay fifty for the rest of her life.

Darren would love to meet Maisie. He is fascinated by history and volunteered himself to be interviewed for The Century Speaks after watching an item on Midlands Today on BBC1. He lives with his mum and dad in an historic toll house just outside Bridgnorth. When I went to see him he had been collecting documents about the building, knew it was constructed around 1820 and could recite the scale of charges levied upon passing traffic. He was also a bit of an authority on the various motoring accidents that had taken place over the years on the road outside, including the one that encroached on his garden. For a twelve year old, Darren had strong and fairly radical views about the future of the motor car and was keen for the government to curb its use. He had never actually been to Villa Park (but taped a heavy hint for posterity that he hoped his Dad would take him soon) and he was not at all happy about the British football scene being dominated by foreign players.

Maisie and Darren were the oldest and youngest. In the past year I have met and interviewed someone born in almost every year between them.

Dorothy Lutner for example arrived on this earth in 1899 and firmly intends to live on it in three separate centuries. She recalls being taken as a little girl to Market Drayton cricket field, there to watch the local blacksmith and bicycle manufacturer attempt to leave the ground in a machine. She remembers people around her saying it was "impossible"... which could have dated the memory to before the Wright Brothers in December 1903. News of their success would otherwise have reached Market Drayton and the crowd would be better informed. But no! Dorothy was adamant she was more than four at the time. And so she was, for when an appeal on Radio Shropshire tracked down the working drawings, they were dated 1908. It turned out to be a vertical take off machine. So Market Drayton is not only the home of gingerbread but also the home of the Harrier Jump Jet.

But what we were particularly after were domestic memories.

One little boy watching a pig killing at Snailbeach in hope of a new bladder for a football was facing up to the disappointment that the doomed animal was a girl pig - because he firmly believed girl pigs do not have bladders.

One little girl (in a family of five) waiting her turn to wear the headphones of the family crystal set was delighted when father realised if he placed the headset in a pudding basin they could all listen at once.

There was also the elderly aunt who watched her niece load the first washing machine in the neighbourhood only to enquire if the clothes have to be washed before you put them in.

Some things, however, never change. It was reassuring to discover that the Young Farmers Clubs of the 1940s were just as much meet, match and marry organisations as they are now ... and that shortly after the electric light was introduced to Oswestry there was a power cut and nobody knew what to do with themselves.

The project brief was not just to interview true born Salopians. I was particularly moved by my interview in Wellington with the first black family in the street. Man's inhumanity to man is still a vivid and recent experience. And I, and a Japanese computer technician in Telford amazed each other with our parallel childhood memories. He tried to describe a traditional Japanese hand game which he believed was only played by children like him in Tokyo in the fifties. I asked him to show me. His eyes widened as I immediately joined in, for "Paper, Scissors, Stone" is clearly more universal than either of us thought. I had always presumed that game was known to only my circle of friends in Manchester in the fifties.

Interestingly, we have also recorded oral history in the making. I was touched by the Regimental Sergeant Major who, because of the late 20th century terrorist threat, had never once been able to wear her uniform home in all her years in the army. And we now have on record for future generations our own growing distrust of the power of supermarkets and our deep disquiet at the advent of genetically modified crops. As one Bishop's Castle resident put it, "Fertilisers were going to feed the world and they didn't; then pesticides were going to feed the world but we got more hunger and more poverty; and now genetic engineering is going to feed the world. Like Hell it is!"

As to the future - there are two camps. The linear camp and the cyclical camp. There are those who see life progressing much as it is already; for ever onwards and upwards. And there are those who believe we are getting too clever by half and would welcome a time to take stock. Time for the pendulum to swing back again towards more traditional values. Darren, who has more future than anyone else featured in this project, is adopting a more pragmatic approach. When aliens arrive in Shropshire he plans to show them the beauty of Cardingmill Valley.

But my lasting impression will be none of the above. Conducting these interviews - as this century becomes the next - what struck me most forcibly is that we no longer seem to have time for each other. To sit down with complete strangers and to share their lives for two hours is enormously enlightening, educating and inspiring. Time after time peace descended upon us as if a gossamer blue blanket had been placed around our shoulders. For two hours the clocks stopped - nobody came to the door - the phone did not ring. We were two strangers suspended in irregular circumstances and delighting in it.

Sadly, this is an age where we have come to view strangers with so much suspicion we are even reluctant to sit down next to one. Think what we are missing. Think of the stories we can tell each other. Think of the life experiences we can share. Think what a waste it is if we do not.

So, for what it's worth, my message to the next century is that we must learn to make time for each other once again.

Chris Eldon Lee

*Dedicated to
the people
of Shropshire*

CHAPTER ONE

WHERE WE LIVE

Shropshire is a county of great diversity and beauty. It has kept families here for generations to continue in its rural traditions. It has inspired poetry, novels and music. It has attracted people to make their home here. There are people who came from Birmingham and the Black Country for work and new housing as the new town of Telford grew and provided a fresh start. There are people who were attracted because of the very remoteness of the rural areas, people who wanted to start their own 'good life', and there are those who were just 'passing through' and stayed.

Gordon Riley sets the scene and explains his love for the county of his birth:

I never moved my home - Shropshire is one of the most beautiful counties. You go to Church Stretton. Do you have to go to Switzerland to see places like that in miniature? Do you have to go to the Lake District? You get the flavour of the Lake District in Ellesmere. There are all sorts of things in this county that still attract me and which have always interested me. There are some things I didn't learn until later on about Shropshire. Although the industrial revolution was said to have started in Coalbrookdale - that wasn't a subject dealt with heavily in my schooldays. I didn't learn that in depth until I went to Telford Development Corporation. All those wonderful things that happened fourteen miles down the road. People in Shropshire are different from those who live in cities - the proud but poor Salopian. You've got to live here about twenty years before they accept you. They are very insular in small ways and very conservative. It's more cosmopolitan now than it was, with people moving into the new town for instance - and not only moving in but coming to work here and not wanting to live where they work, so they've radiated out from the industrial area of Shropshire.

Gordon Riley b. 1922

Beryl Gower explains how she felt about moving here from Norwich:

In 1936 I realised there was a lovely town called Shrewsbury with all these wonderful rolling hills. My husband applied for a post up here when the Wakeman school was due to open and the Education Authority decided they wanted a grammar school

1

for both sexes - a co-ed grammar for the whole of the county - not just for the town - with all the facilities for the sciences, proper workshops for metalwork, wood work and jewellery making. His interview lasted three days - it was terrible for us at home, me and my sons waiting for news - then he rang up one evening and said "I've got the job!" We were in Norwich right over in the East. I was excited about coming here because I had already read about Shropshire and it sounded a wonderful town - a town so close to the Welsh border countryside and, having read the Mary Webb books helped me to envisage Shropshire. Although I loved it in Norwich, it's a cathedral city and pretty hectic, but Shrewsbury was the most wonderful town, with all the church spires and of course then, unspoilt with the modern shops. My husband loved his job, and we keep in touch with a lot of the staff and students.

Beryl Gower b. 1918

I remember saying when I was in the Army "I come from Shropshire" and people would say "Where's that?" which I thought was encouraging.

John Oliver b. 1929

John and Jackie Gunton moved into Shropshire to become self sufficient:

The first step was to buy this land. It was just a field with planning permission for a caravan about a mile away from Prees Heath. We bought a caravan and we were able to buy this place for cash on the profit of the house we sold. We started cultivating largely based on the idea of self sufficiency. We thought "Well, we'll be able to grow most things for ourselves, we won't need much of an income." We had a certain amount of savings to keep us going for the first two or three years at a fairly low level, and then we thought we'd make a little bit of money just to make up the difference, but it's worked out completely differently. You need a lot of money to survive, even at a low level. Making an income off the land is exceedingly difficult and we've ended up really being market gardeners rather than self sufficient people.

John Gunton b. 1945

I came here in the seventies. I had a short holiday here and came to Ludlow in the autumn - it was absolutely superb. I fell in love with the scenery. Then I came back in 1980 and this place was for sale - a derelict cottage with land ... I fell in love with the

2

place, the lovely rich soil, and I thought, "I'll give it a whirl".
It was like going back into the late 1800s, 1900s. It was beautiful.
It still is beautiful but it's changed, the rural aspect of it.

What in 20 years?

Oh tremendously, when I moved here it was all small farms and smallholdings. Nearly every house was a local person or someone with a local connection. Now they are mostly 'incomers', commuters, and the really local people are being edged out.

How do you feel about having a role to play in that process?

Because I've worked here I let myself off the hook a bit.
It [this cottage] would have just been sold as a pocket of land but I've built it up again as a smallholding and I'm quite proud I've done that. This is an organic holding and I hope when I leave somebody will carry that on. I know I'll never be local. I'll always be an 'incomer'.

What about your daughter?

She'll always be an 'incomer' even though she was born and raised here.

Polly Bolton b. 1950

I was born down Lion Lane in a little village called
The Knowle at the foot of the Clee Hill. I've only
moved a mile in seventy years!

Dennis Crowther b. 1926

The best I can describe [living on the Clee Hill] is on a summer's night when you drive home and you cross the cattle grid.
It's the equivalent of being on holiday. No matter what sort of day you've had, no matter what time of day, if it's a nice blue sky and you drive over that cattle grid and you've got that view, everything else just pales into insignificance ... the hustle and the bustle is gone and it's just peace and tranquillity.

Dave Smart b. 1958

In the 1990s it seems that communities are resurrecting themselves and Castlefields has taken on a new lease of life:

Castlefields is a wonderful area. It's Shrewsbury's 'muesli' belt, where the late sixties people came to live. We decided we'd all stay here and get old together. It's good fun being together with our neighbours - a good community. When something happens to somebody here, people rally round and support each other - people care. I feel I can be a gay man in this neighbourhood and nobody's really going to give a damn.

Geoff Hardy b. 1950 ———

3

Broseley is a small friendly town where you can get to know people. I'm very fortunate to be in this close with seventeen houses in it because we really are quite a little community. We have all sorts of parties. One about Christmas and one about midsummer. We have a 90 year old man and the youngest is a baby about 18 months. We all mix very well together despite our different backgrounds.

Vera Smith b. 1916

Over the century there have been enormous changes to the communities in Shropshire. Jonathon Hayward reflects on these in the village where he grew up and where he and his family still live:

Brockton was very much a declining community at that time in the 1950s and early 60s. The only other children in the village went away to school. I was in the state school sector and I think I was the only person under thirty-five in the village for quite some time, which was a rather strange thing to think back to. I certainly view it more positively now we have a lot more children in the village. Having been an only child, I was determined not to have an only child.

Jon Hayward b. 1951

Jon went away to university but returned to the farm on the death of his father:

I came back out of a sense of duty more than anything else, not because of a love of farming. I had had a varied life prior to that. In retrospect I'm glad I did because the way agriculture has gone it hasn't been the job for life I thought it was. I hadn't got the experience someone who had never left the farm would have had. I had a very steep learning curve without anyone around to teach me. There was assistance from the Ministry of Agriculture and neighbours were helpful. My grandfather's experience was no longer relevant by that stage because he came from a previous horse husbandry environment.

Jon Hayward b. 1951

In the north of the county Mary Hignett describes Oswestry in the 1920s:

The Oswestry I remember was a very small town compared to how it is today. Most of the people were either shopkeepers or worked on the railways. There were long terraces of houses built by private developers for railway people, and it was the done thing to provide enough garden for the father to grow food for the family. Because the houses were all close together the gardens had to be long and narrow. I remember these particularly. Most of them were not worked but were bare earth [by my time]. The people were doing a good days work at the railway works and I think they felt they'd had enough by then. I never saw grass there at all ... I think the reason was that the only way to cut grass in those days was with a scythe and few of the fathers knew how to scythe grass. In Cae Glas Park they had sheep to cut the grass.

Mary Hignett b. 1912

In the south of the county Evelyn Hatton described her feeling of continuity with the county:

We came from Wolverhampton to Pontesbury when I was five, to a little cottage in Linley Terrace. To get there you had to go up past the cemetery where there were just fields or up Habberley Road which was just as lonely then. For my mum it must have been very traumatic, but we went back with my dad, his family had lived in Pontesbury for generations. Challinors and Pontesbury go together. Someone said, "if you stood in Pontesbury and shouted Challinor they'd come from all directions". The cottage looked right out over Pontesford hill where we used to go to play for hours. You could go up there without being afraid then.

Evelyn Hatton b. 1926

Ashford Carbonell has altered for the better, according to Margaret Jones:

The village has changed out of this world. We've got new houses, extra school buses. We've got a sports field which we didn't have. The Village Hall has been adapted and modernised - a ramp and things like that - a car park. The car park used to be the allotment during the war. We've still got our school for which we're very lucky, a lot of schools have closed. We've still got our church. The Methodist Church closed many, many years ago. I miss the farmers bringing their cattle and sheep down the road, you don't see that now, that part of village life has gone. There are new houses and people from the bottom of the village who you wave at in the car but you haven't a clue who they are because they keep coming and going.

Margaret Jones b. 1926

I like Shropshire very much, it's a very large county ... virtually two really - the north and the south divided by the River Severn ... it's by and large untouched. Fortunately the major development happened in Telford and has to a degree been 'islanded' by motorways - it hasn't contaminated the countryside too much. There's a road which epitomises Shropshire [to me] that leads from Shrewsbury via Ratlinghope down to Bishop's Castle. That road, apart from the surface, wouldn't have changed since mediaeval times. You can go down there and see nothing that's modern. It's a beautiful road.

Michael Raven b. 1938

In 1964 the face of Shropshire changed forever with the building of the new town of Telford. Gordon Riley gives the background:

I was one of the editorial team that founded 'The Shropshire Star'. We were the first industry to start up in the new town in 1964. I was dealing with the roots of Telford (as a journalist with the paper) from its very start. The influx of Brummies provided diametrically opposed people to the grass roots people. Telford - when it started as Dawley New Town - was to handle the overspill of Birmingham. The overspill is one of those code words to describe the people who lived in the back to back tunnel type dwellings. They had a different culture, different humour, different accent and had done different jobs. There were the five towns there, all very proud of their history and traditions. So much so that Wellington, being the market town, was a higher social strata than Oakengates - which was iron, Dawley which was coal and to some degree Madeley and Ironbridge. The people that were coming liked their booze, the riotous noise of their entertainment and they somehow couldn't understand the people they were coming to dwell amongst but part of that was caused by the majority of the people in East Shropshire who called them usurpers and didn't want them.

Gordon Riley b. 1922

Telford didn't impinge on my life at all. I've been to Telford once in my life.

Brian Barrett b. 1929

Kathleen Hann was born in the Black Country and as one of the people coming into Shropshire explains her feelings about moving into the county:

We kept a pub in the Black Country and were fed up of working 25 hours a day, 8 days a week. We saw in the 'Express and Star' there were houses to let in Telford. God's country. My husband applied. He came on his own because I had to run the pub. He arrived about seven in the morning and somebody told him

to go up Oakengates where the labour exchange was.
They told him there were only two places he could get a job -
up at Donnington with the Army - and he didn't want that because
he'd been in the Navy most of his life - and the other was Sankeys -
so he went to Sankeys. To have a house, you'd got to have a job
earning £20 a week - that was the rule then. There were no benefits.
Anyway he went to Sankeys and told the manager he'd got to have
a job earning £20 a week and he had to wait a month because
he had to put in a month's notice on the pub. The manager
promised to keep him a job at £20 a week. While he was working
his notice out, Sankeys went on strike and we were scared we
thought we'd loose the house and the job. The strikers went
back the day he started work - and he started with a 10% rise.
From then on - 29 years ago - it's been heaven!

The rent was £9 16/- a week for the house from TDC.
We had a 3 bedroomed house on Sutton Hill which we thought
was heaven. It was the very first place to be built, Sutton Hill.
Well, the walls were still damp when we moved in. My husband
was working hard but we felt we were on holiday. I said, "I'm
not going to work, I've done enough work, I'm going to relax."
Then after about three weeks I got a job. But it still feels like
we're on holiday even after nearly thirty years.

Her welcome to Shropshire was not assured:

People resented us. Madeley was destroyed. If I'd have been a
local in Madeley, I'd have been at the front of the queue protesting.
I can understand it. As they went on doing other places they
were more considerate I think. Telford's done a lot of good.

Kathleen Hann b. 1930

I never write Telford on my letters. I put the address,
postcode and Shropshire.

Della Bailey b. 1928

Telford has its supporters:

I worked in Telford and I think it's a pretty good place actually.
As a new town they've really worked quite hard to make it attractive.
The roads to the centre are quite good. It's light and it's airy and
they've tried to create as many amenities as they can. There's still
a huge amount missing for young people - there's not enough
transport to get people from one facility to another - or home.
I'm very glad not to be living in Telford but I think it's very useful.
It's brought a lot of people to the area and a lot of employment.

Ruth Walmsley b. 1943

I love Telford. I don't live in it but I still have many ties. It was a difficult concept and I'm not sure it was fundamentally right at its outset but I think it has been a success, particularly now that Telford and Wrekin have got unitary status. I think we'll see an even stronger bonding of the whole town. There are still elements of difficulty - the 'us' and 'them'. And there are the market towns that I think have suffered as a result of Telford Town Centre and out of town supermarkets, but that isn't just a specific Telford problem. If you look at Telford, it's become strong.

Jo Havell b. 1943

... and its detractors:

Telford is very useful and they work very hard with the trees and grass and flowers to make the whole place palatable - but it's still a blot on the landscape. However you look at it, it shouldn't be there ... I'm not a great lover of Telford.

Mary Stone b. 1932

My father didn't like the 'New Town'. He didn't like it taking the greenery because he loved the countryside. He used to say, "Soon you'll have to take a five mile bike ride to see a field".

Della Bailey b. 1928

Telford Development Corporation (TDC) had their dreams and plans for making the new population into a community. Given the diversity of the original five towns which had provided the basis for Telford, it looked like it was going to be a long haul:

You'd never find a Wellington girl bringing home a prospective husband from Dawley - and you wouldn't get Oakengates and Dawley mixing together. Dawley lads would go down to Ironbridge or Bridgnorth to find their wives. This is the difficulty we've got. It will take a long time to make it a whole town - generations.

Gordon Riley b. 1922

Little progress was made until the' Shropshire Star' printed an article about one of the new Telford estates:

The article branded Sutton Hill because of the number of divorces (they'd got the statistics from somewhere) and the headline read "Sutton Hill - Sin City". That had an amazing affect. Rather than the rest of the town ganging up on them because of the article, the community within Sutton Hill - I think it was 44 little groups - sprung up from the residents to show they weren't 'Sin City' after all. An adverse headline brought

about good and started to weld the incoming population together.
When the town park was established people started to meet
each other in the park and in the town centre as it was developing,
and it somehow started to gel.

Gordon Riley b. 1922

> **As far as Telford is concerned I think they just didn't
> think about how to create communities at all.
> They built a lot of houses and everything else just came
> along as an afterthought. If communities did spring up
> it was more by good luck than good management.**
>
> **Katherine Soutar b. 1963**

*Katherine describes her feelings about Woodside in Telford.
She moved to Telford when she was seven:*

Woodside when we first moved there was like a little island.
All around it were ponds and fields and waste ground that you
could explore ... I remember collecting seventy toads in one day
and then being told to let them all go again!

Katherine Soutar b. 1963 ———

*Lynne Scott remembers the beginnings of Telford from her
work on the inside:*

I was at college and applied to Telford Development Corporation
at eighteen. I got the job and worked in the typing pool for five
years. You got to know everything that was going on in every
department. I felt my job was part of a team that was actually
making changes to people's lives and I used to really enjoy it.
I loved going to work, wondering what was going to happen today.
Having known the place for so long you'd be given a piece of
work and suddenly realise there in front of you was what was
going to happen to this piece of land. And as you were working
on it you could picture what it was going to be like.

I remember when they first talked about the Town Park and
the great Giant they were going to have in Wonderland. It was
just amazing ... the best thing that's ever happened to us. I think
it was very pioneering, with lots of young people involved just
out of university and wanting to make their mark in their chosen
professions. It was a strong young go-ahead team.

But there was a concern over the first houses that were being
built. I remember going to the opening at Sutton Hill and we'd
expected something wonderful. But when we got there I thought,
" I don't like these at all". Everybody was very proud of them at

9

the time, but as time went on and new housing was built you'd hear people say, "Well, we must make sure we don't make the same mistakes again."

Lynn Scott b. 1954

Dave Smart moved to the Clees but works outside Shropshire:

Sue goes to work at about a quarter to eight. I go out before or just after. She gets back at 4.30 - 5.30, I get back at 6 to 6.30. It's difficult to get involved in the local community. We have been to certain functions that were put on down in Cleobury, down in Ludlow, but I wouldn't say we were part of the community. I would say that we were residents in the area. My wife still does her shopping in Kidderminster - occasionally she goes down to Hereford. We do bits of shopping in Cleobury and Ludlow, so we bring some wealth to the community. But not as much as the locals do. We don't use the local facilities that much - we don't use the library. We used to ask advice at the local post office - but since it's moved we've not been in. We use local firms. I think I belong here as much as anybody else. It doesn't bother me whether I am involved in the community. I always vote and answer questionnaires sent round by the Parish. The one that came round recently - should there be protected cheap accommodation to ... keep the young people within the area and I think there should. I don't think you should drive people away from the community that they are brought up in if they don't want to go.

Dave Smart b. 1958

Dennis Crowther illustrated his thoughts:

They've come from the city now - with their city ways. Nice people but they've come with their ways and it dunna fit in. They'll walk straight by the country inn where we have our social activities, to go out and have a meal - when there's plenty of food in the house to eat!

Dennis Crowther b. 1926

Fred Jordan lives in the tiny village of Aston Munslow and he reflected on the different types of people who had moved in to his locality:

I feel very much part of the local community, but there's only my neighbours and two more in the village that are village folks. The others are all fresh folks. Some are good - there's a young policeman just bought a cottage and done it up nicely, he's got a wife and two nice little kids, and the people on the new building plot are good neighbours, but some of them I don't even know. There's two good houses owned by people who are only weekenders - two wasted gardens gone to rack and ruin. They never go to the shop or the pub.

Fred Jordan b. 1922

Evelyn Hatton, from the rural community in Pontesbury remarked on some of the changes:

I don't approve of the changes in Shropshire really. Our village, it was like a big family, you knew everybody that lived there and all the different houses. Mind you, having said that, the lane I lived in ... was just a little lane that went up with hedges both sides. Well, we had our bungalow built up there, so we spoilt it really, when you think about it. Ours was built second, and then there were others. The lane was unspoilt and then there were the bungalows.

Evelyn Hatton b. 1926

Margaret Jones reflects on the 'incomers' in the village of Ashford Carbonell in a positive light:

The new people in the village work outside and away from it. People used to work in the village or in Ludlow. These are away and you don't get to know them so well as you used to. Some commute to Birmingham. This did dilute the spirit of the village, but we've now got a village hall committee with an extremely good chairman and she's getting it all together again. It's wonderful. They're having trips to go to the opera and plays and things. She's an 'incomer', but she's more than welcome. It used to be if you hadn't been here for thirty years you weren't accepted, but that's all gone now - it's another thing that's gone. You just say, "Oh there's somebody else coming - who is it?"... I doubt if there's more than eight people in the village that have been here for a long time, the rest of the village is made up of newcomers, so the resistance to newcomers has gone. You've got to accept them - the majority are for it.

Margaret Jones b. 1926

People who have come to live in Shropshire perhaps become more the Proud Salopian:

We came to Shropshire twenty-four years ago. I am absolutely a Shropshire person. I've lived here longer than I've lived anywhere. I came here originally by agreeing to take a job for a minimum of three years and I didn't intend to stay but Shropshire caught me. It's in my blood and I absolutely love it.

Jo Havell b. 1943

Jo feels she has been accepted now:

The people in Shropshire are friendly immediately, then they take a while to really know you and accept you. Then suddenly you find - I don't know how it happens - they're investing you with quite considerable trust and they'll share anything with you. They'll take risks in what they say to you and you realise you've been accepted. I have some lovely people in Broseley who now assume my father was a native of Broseley, although he can't ever have been. In a way they make the assumption, and that is their way of saying you're now of us.

Jo Havell b. 1943

I'll tell you what I think stops people being so friendly and mixing is that little bit of metal ... you get into a car and drive everywhere, you don't wait at the bus stop, you don't talk to people and children are afraid to.

Della Bailey b. 1928

Although now resident in Worcestershire Richard Blythe still sees Shropshire as his true home:

I always look at the Shrewsbury football results first ...
I love the top of the Wrekin ... in winter or summer. It must have been a very significant place for the tribes that lived in the area ... perhaps I get some good vibes up there. I took my granddaughter up there and I like the continuity.

Richard Blythe b.1926

Ruth Walmsley was excited at the prospect of moving into the country:

I was brought up in suburban London and had this image of what it must be like to be brought up on a farm. I was absolutely delighted (when I moved to Shropshire) with the fact that I lived in the country - I couldn't believe this fantasy was going to be a reality and I started to explore locally, Benthall Woods etcetera and I just loved it. I still feel terribly excited by the fact that I'm not visiting here, that I live in this most beautiful county. And then once we discovered the Long Mynd well then that was it, could we ever leave Shropshire?

Ruth Walmsley b 1943

Perhaps Shrewsbury wasn't quite so pleasant years ago:

We had herds of cattle going up the Cop and they'd tend to run up the passages each side. It was all jolly dirty. The Cop was steaming and filthy, on market days particularly. And these cows on their way to the Smithfield would very often take fright - Compasses Passage on the Cop was a favourite spot for a great big bull to get stuck in. The poor animal, it was so narrow it couldn't get out.

Was there any effort made to clear up afterwards?

We used to have a water cart come round and spray water and I think the council came round with brooms, but on the whole it was pretty smelly.

Marie Kelly b. 1914

Living in an old house in Bridgnorth has given Darren an interest in history:

This house was a toll house. My dad's researched it quite a bit and he got someone to look for information about it. It took the tolls on the old Worcester Road and the new road ... we do know they only kept each toll keeper for ten years in case they went a bit funny about collecting money or anything like that.

Darren Fountain b. 1987

Once ensconced in Shropshire the new arrivals quickly blended in and became almost prouder of their adopted home than the natives of the county. Beryl Gower takes up the story of the changes which took place in her part of Shrewsbury:

Since we've been here we've seen about two to three thousand houses built but we are a happy little community here. But not in the way perhaps communities were when we were younger. I remember the Radbrook Hotel as a private house and the owner had his horse and carriages - there's the coach house down in the hollow where the brook is and the white building opposite the hotel is where the servants lived. Every night at 7 o'clock I heard the bagpipes playing before his dinner. They played outside his house. The gardens came right down to this corner with three fountains, a Chinese garden, a Japanese garden, an Italian garden and two English gardens. We saw all that vanish and all the houses go up.

Beryl Gower b. 1918

We went to Happy Valley and paddled. There was no fear of anybody attacking in those days - It was lovely ... I went there a couple of years ago. It isn't the same because they've planted trees on it. When I was young, Pontesford Hill was smooth with just a mane of trees, Scotch pine I think they were, right down the middle. It was the shape of a lion and the little hill we always called the head.

The saddest change in Pontesbury is to see those empty shops - they were all family businesses. To think how they started- the boss my uncle Bert was started off in his business by the Reverend Ewbank and then he bought it himself in later years. Uncle Bert learnt his trade as a baker at Bennets. When he opened his shop, he used to go round all the villages. They went even as far as Welshpool everyday with bread, all round Longden, Westbury, all up the Bridges, Hugleth, Habberley. He used to go and get orders, his sisters worked for him in the shop and the girl he was going to marry. He'd bake the bread himself, the girls used to put the orders up and he used to deliver them, all on his own. He deserved to get on didn't he? ... Now that shop is empty.

Evelyn Hatton b. 1926

Jon Hayward explains how he and his wife were setting about rebuilding their local community:

A lot of the revitalisation has been because of new people coming into Corvedale and building new houses or renovating old ones and realising it was a nice place to live. When we came back in 1978 there was nothing tying that community together and Sue and some of the other young mums in the area decided to form a mother and toddler club in the village hall at Shipton which is just a mile down the road. It proved very popular and continues to this day as a place where young parents can go with their children and share experiences because the countryside can be a very lonely place as the town can - particularly when you've got a small child.

Jon Hayward b. 1951

Richard Beaumond described the alterations to his birthplace:

I was thinking only the other day as I looked out from the top of the church tower where I'd put the flag up for Good Friday, half mast of course, and then you have to go up again on Sunday to put it to the top of the mast. But I always pause for a little look round and I was reminded of John Arlott's reply when he was asked how Basingstoke had changed since his boyhood there and he said "It was simply not the same place". It wasn't necessarily better or worse it was just a different place. And actually, so is Lydbury North. If you look down now from the church tower most of the field boundaries have changed. Where there used to be half a dozen little patchwork meadows, there's now one minor prairie. Most of the cottage gardens that in my youth provided enough vegetables for a family throughout the year became lawns in the sixties. Then there were the building plots of the eighties. So the pattern of the village has changed. Whereas it once grouped itself along the road that runs east-west and up and down the brook that runs north-south, the bungalows now uniformly face south. The gardens are of a fairly regular shape and we have the standard pattern of leylandii marking out the divisions between one little piece of territory and another. On Sunday mornings we're drowned by the sound of lawn mowers, same as everybody else.

Richard Beaumond b. 1948

Alan J Gardner learnt about Shropshire in his geography class:

In geography our teacher would draw on the blackboard an outline of the British mainland and first of all we'd have to fill in the rivers, right from the Thames, round the south of England, up the coast to the Mersey and up the western side of the country. Then with the broad side of the chalk the teacher would mark in the hill masses as we called them out. Right from the south of England - the South Downs, the North Downs, the Mendips, right up to the north of England finishing with the Cheviots. Then at the very end she would take the pointed end of the chalk and mark a dot in the middle of the map and we'd all say, "And the Wrekin". Many years later I got my first glimpse of the Wrekin when I was travelling up from London to The Lakes by train and between Birmingham and Stafford, I was looking out of the window to the west and I saw a hill and I thought "That must be the Wrekin!" I got quite excited.

Years later my son and I were working for the GEC installing the railway signalling for the Ironbridge Power Station. On the first Sunday he and I went up the Wrekin. It was late February but it was a beautifully mild day and whilst we were sitting on the top rocks a butterfly settled close to us. It must have been brought out by the warmth of the day. But we had snow later and Shropshire suddenly became a black and white county.

Alan J Gardner b. 1912

Sadly, the stories about local people not being able to afford local houses is the same the country over:

I was born at Crow's Nest, Snailbeach, in the same house my father was born in. But strangers live there now. Snailbeach is not Snailbeach anymore. Since they had the water and the electric and all that, new people have come in and bought the cottages. They'd give a terrible price so our youngsters could no longer afford them They're all in council houses at Minsterley.

Molly Rowson b. 1908

For Elaine Bruce it was memories that drew her to Shropshire:

I wanted to live in a small place. I wanted to be near the country, but not buried in the country. I needed to have cheaper housing and this place had some childhood memories of being a staging post on our way to Wales from Cheshire. It was a good place to come. I had a childhood memory of Clun - a picture of green rolling hills.

Elaine Bruce b. 1938

Conversely, while Mary Stone was blissfully happy on her Shropshire Hill she had this to say about Ludlow:

I didn't like Ludlow. It's a pretty town but there seemed to be a tremendous difference in social attitude between Ludlow and the people around me in Bucknell. There seemed to be a tremendous sense of class and status. People would accept that they were somehow below other people based entirely on where they went to school ... a woman parked on the Buttercross and a traffic warden went to point out that she was blocking three roads. She turned to him with a stentorian voice and said, "Don't you know who I am my good man?"... those social attitudes are absolutely risible

Mary Stone b. 1932

She also came across the question of an address with an attached stigma:

When I was working with the YTS (Youth Training Scheme) there was a girl with ten top grade GCSEs and she came to me (she'd applied for a job in the tax office, I think) and asked if she could use my address - I asked her why and she said, "I'm off the Sandpits Estate in Ludlow, and they won't even answer it if it's that address." To my horror the other students agreed. So she used my address and got the job.

Mary Stone b. 1932

Bridgnorth is quite straight laced and stiff upper lip but I was young and the young people were great, but you had a lot of the English violence thing. The Highley crowd would come to Bridgnorth - and the Broseley crowd - and there'd be a battle. Apparently it had been even worse before. I didn't get involved particularly.

Squirrel b. 1951

And of course there may be a little eccentricity around. Malcolm Booth's family picnics must have been interesting to watch:

On winter Sundays my wife would prepare a hotpot meal and as soon as church was over we'd get in the car and go out to The Breiddens to have a picnic. Quite often we'd surprise walkers who'd come over the brow of the hill to see the Booth family having lunch in splendid isolation in often very cold conditions.

Malcolm Booth b. 1924

but there again ...

For well over twenty years we've had our Christmas lunch on the top of The Wrekin. When my parents-in-law died we were left without a natural venue for Christmas Day lunch and we decided we ought to do something different. Just to have Christmas lunch on our own didn't seem terribly attractive so we started to take a picnic up The Wrekin. It's had its moments. Shirley Tart wrote in her column in 'The Shropshire Star' that we would be having lunch on The Wrekin. The following day a very grand lady came up to us and said "Are you the people who lunch on The Wrekin?", and her eyes swept round imperiously trying to find the field kitchen which should have been cooking the turkey. But we have done it for years and now quite a lot of other people join us. We take some mulled wine and share a glass of that and enjoy it immensely.

In all weathers?

We've never not gone because of the weather. One year it was incredibly bitterly cold but we've never had so much snow that we couldn't go.

Judge Michael Mander b. 1936

> **There are old lead mines up there too [Stapeley Hill] and we were told not to go in there in case the headless monster got us! The Roman lead mines had tunnels in the side of the hill - in some places about three foot high.**
>
> **Terry Tandler b. 1951**

We do as we've always done here, we sit astride the border, neither of Wales nor of England.

Is it uncomfortable sitting across the Welsh border?

Not now - nor has it been I suspect, for several generations. But if you look a little bit deeper over the hedges and in the copses and fields you see the sort of signs that clearly identify the Welsh Marches as the Bosnia of five or six hundred years ago. Border castles, forts, little emplacements, signs of the tribal strife of the day, thankfully well buried now. Although the ancient rivalries are regularly re-enacted in some sort of proscribed, produced and directed forum, such as sport.

Richard Beaumond, b 1948

Judge Michael Mander moved into Garmston:

Garmston is a little hamlet. Ours was the eleventh property in it - there are now three times as many after 35 years - and was very obviously the first new property for a hundred years. So it was a very attractive place to live.

What sort of reaction was there locally when you came in and started building the first house in the village for a hundred years?

In those days there wasn't the controversy there would be today. And at that time my wife's father was the rector of the village in which we were building the house. Now, Garmston has become a satellite dormitory village for Telford. There isn't much employment and there aren't many people in Garmston who work in the village. When we first came here I would think everybody worked no further away than Wellington, now many work in the West Midlands and travel everyday. When we moved here there would be many functions in the local village halls, now there are very few indeed because that's not the sort of entertainment that people are looking for. Village entertainment tends to be very unsophisticated. People's expectations have been raised by television.

Judge Michael Mander b. 1936

There's something about Shropshire. It grows on you. There's a nice mixture of country and town. There's a slower tempo of life and the history of the place envelops you.

Malcolm Booth b. 1924

The last word:

All the children were blissfully happy in Shropshire. Everyone had the feeling, "you've come home", that this was where you were meant to be - this was the best place on earth.

Mary Stone b. 1932

CHAPTER 2
HOUSE AND HOME

One of the greatest changes we have seen over the century is to our houses, our homes. At the beginning of the century the privy was down the bottom of the garden, there was a pig in a sty, possibly some chickens too and a space for growing vegetables. As things moved on and the some of the rural locations became swallowed by the towns, standards changed. Indoor plumbing became usual, gardens disappeared, the landscape changed and people began to have their own bedrooms rather than sharing with a multitude of brothers and sisters. Half a century ago, 10% of houses were without electricity and 33 % had no fixed bath. Now these things are seen as necessities rather than luxuries. More people became owner occupiers and housing came to be considered not only as accommodation but a source of wealth and status. Now the TV shows us endless home design programmes, incorporating the gardens too and do-it-yourself is a boom market.

In this chapter we hear from people who remember the past, the tiny cottages sleeping five to a bedroom, the outdoor privy and the slum clearances in Shrewsbury. How have things moved on and changed?

Times haven't changed quite so much for Fred Jordan who still lives in a two down and one up cottage in Aston Munslow:

> On Saturday morning I get the bath and I get the hot water from the boiler, put it in front of the fire and I have a good wash. I always wash in soft water, rainwater from the tank, you get a good lather on that. The mains water is all limestone like, you can't get a good wash with it, its too hard.

Despite what might be seen as privations in his home Fred enjoys his life there:

> My cottage was condemned and they wanted to turn me out because someone on the council wanted it. I went to the Squire and he said, "We won't have you turned out". He did get them to say I can live here as long as I want but I mustn't sell it. I've no intention of selling it. They offered me £300 - compulsory purchase - and I said, "Get down that road - £300 wouldn't buy a fowl house! You could build three houses here."

Fred Jordan b.1922

21

Wem in 1946 was a very sleepy town. It was derelict in places really because of the war. Nothing had been done to it. We hadn't got main sewerage in a lot of houses. Instead we had the night-soil cart two or three times a week ... and if your windows were open you shut them quick because the smell was terrible. We had main drainage in this house but the cottages down the road hadn't. They didn't even have an indoor loo.

Why did the cart come at night?

So that we couldn't see what was what! They went into the back door picked up the bucket and chucked it into the cart and hoped people wouldn't see. If you had a party you made sure your guests left before ten to twelve at night, otherwise they were likely to land on the doorstep as the wretched contraption came up the road.

**Dr John Keeling-Roberts b. 1916 and
Margaret Keeling-Roberts b. 1919**

Richard Blythe even pressed his dog into service when it came to bath time:

I moved to Montford Bridge with my wife into a terraced council house, the end house. This would be in 1952 ... There was no toilet; there was a bath but no water - there was a conduit and we had to carry water. I had a Labrador dog and he used to carry the empty buckets out and I carried the full ones back. It was seven buckets for a bath - we had to put the water in the copper, heat it up, take it out of the copper and put it in the bath. My wife and I struggled there for quite some time before the Atcham District Authority put water and an inside toilet into the houses.

Richard Blythe b.1926

Some had a little more help:

My grandfather, at the age of eleven, went out to Gatacre Hall (just beyond Bridgnorth) into service. He didn't come home again until he was fifteen. Four years and he never came home. He was in service in the house because my grandmother kept the pub. He was a gentleman's gentleman and travelled all over the place.

John Oliver b.1929

John and Margaret Oliver found their dream house in a Shrewsbury suburb just after they were married:

We got married in 1956 and lived for a year with Margaret's parents. We were trying to find a house where we could keep bees. Housing was quite difficult to find at that time. We wanted to be near Shrewsbury because of work. My sister had a music teacher who lived here. She'd known her years and they were great friends. I happened to say to my sister, "That's a nice house - I wouldn't mind living there". She mentioned it to the music teacher who said, "Tell John to make me an offer". I said, "Don't be ridiculous I couldn't possibly afford that place". The message came back - "Never mind that - tell him to make me an offer he can afford". It meant getting a mortgage, and all we had to play with was £3000 and it was worth a lot more than that. She accepted the offer. She said, "If I sell it for more, I'll go into a higher band of death duties". So we had what the Exchequer didn't have!

John and Margaret Oliver b.1929

Vicky Cowell was taken aback when she discovered what she had taken for little factories turned out to be houses:

I came here to live in 1959. I left Jamaica on 25th March 1959 and landed here on the 26th. My husband came to meet me. Travelling in London on the tube, I noticed all the way there were factories. Well I thought they were, because in Jamaica the only thing with chimneys on the top were factories. I said to him, "Where are all the houses, I haven't seen anything coming along but factories - people must have a lot of work". He laughed but he didn't say anything. We came on the train to Wellington and I kept seeing the chimneys so I said, "Where are the houses then?" So he says, "You'll soon see where you're going". We used to live near Union Street in Wellington ... It's all different now, there were some old buildings there. We went to no. 51 Victoria Avenue and I said, "why are we going into this factory?" and he said, "It's not a factory, it's the house".

Vicky Cowell b.1931

Gordon Riley's parents moved up a bracket into the home owning community:

Having been living in a two up two down with a lavatory outside in Copthorne, there came an opportunity for my parents to buy their own house. They hit upon a bungalow in Monkmoor which was part of the old RAF station in the first World War. They liked the idea of being property owners. There was a stumbling block. The cost was £150. The deposit was £25 which was quite a struggle to raise, but they eventually did.

It was a typical service building - one long building which had been divided into two - it had a sitting room, two bedrooms, a bathroom with hot water and a living room with a big fireplace. It was very grand for someone who had arrived from a two up two down with no hot water and one of those old brown sinks. We had gaslight in Copthorne Rise but the bungalow we went to wasn't on the gas or electricity mains. It had running water but not drinking water. I had to fetch it in pails from a stand pipe.

Gordon Riley b.1922

Margaret Jones' home in Ashford Carbonell seemed to have a sitting tenant:

I had to have the house exorcised. After my mother died we decided to move into this side of the house and have the other side decorated. We went up to the bedroom, it was very hot weather in 1974 but we couldn't get into the bedroom. It was like walking into ice. Nothing was floating. Nothing was seen, but we just couldn't get in ... so we left it and in the end we called in a medium ... she'd got short hair and it just shot up on end and she said, "I can't go in there!" So we thought it was time we called a priest. We called in an exorcist and he went bell, book and candle in every room in the house. He said, "Your mother is such a strong person she didn't want to leave. There's no harm, she just didn't want to leave the house". Two days later the whole house was quiet and we've had no trouble since.

Margaret Jones b.1926

But there are still unwelcome visitors in the lane:

This house is on a ley line. Actually ley lines were groups of big grey stone which used to be signposts in the old days. They can be 20 miles apart, 70 miles apart, 100 miles apart and people used to walk from one to the other to get to different places. Now at 2 o'clock every morning there's a group of what they call 'memories', and they walk past and say, "Yea brethren, I'll meet thee at the Host House". I found out that the "host house" was a safe house during the Civil War, so I presume they were going to a safe house, running away from somewhere. You can hear them, you can't see them. The same thing every morning at 2 am, and I'm fed up with them - every day since the 1960s, my husband heard them as well.

Margaret Jones b.1926

Houses were very different in Jamaica:

In the room we rented in Wellington I saw this big fireplace.
I'd never seen a fireplace in a bedroom, a coal fire. I'd come at
the end of March, when the winter was just going off and my
husband said, "You have to make a fire". "In the house?" I said.
And he said "Well, that's the way to warm you."

Vicky Cowell b.1931

Ron Miles gives a vivid description of where he lived as a child:

The first house I lived in was 65 Lloyds Head in Jackfield.
It's gone now. It was facing the river in the heart of Jackfield.
I was born in 1929. The house was minute with two rooms
down and two rooms up. Downstairs were the kitchen or living
room and the back kitchen with a sloping roof. A tiny little room
with a little Coalbrookdale fire grate in the corner - that was the
living room. In another corner was what you called a stair foot
door and you went up a winding staircase and into the one
bedroom above. That was my mother and father's bedroom.
Then there was a tiny little room with a lean to at the back and
that was for my brother and I to sleep in. It was so small my brother
was farmed out. It was quite common. He went to live over the
river with my mother's auntie in Madeley Wood. She brought him
up so I suppose I had more room. There was a tin bath hanging
up on the back kitchen wall and the toilet was up the garden.
Square sheets of newspaper hung on a nail on a white washed
wall, a tin of tar in the corner with a brush in it to keep it smelling
sweet. Of course the seats were scrubbed so there was a soapy
smell. There was one wooden seat - none of this two seats business.
Not like Madeley Wood where they were another class altogether!
There was a bucket underneath and that was emptied by the
night soil collector. I think he came round on a Monday morning.

Ron Miles b.1929

*It wasn't all bliss inheriting Linley Hall despite the difference
in location and size:*

When Lady Moore died I moved into Sir Jasper's dressing room,
and I noticed there was a terrible sag in the ceiling. When I went
up, there was a small mushroom factory up there! A dog's dish
was catching water from a hole in the roof and nothing had been
done about it for a very long time. Also, when the builders got to
work they found a bees' nest I hadn't noticed. So at great expense
I had the bees moved by the builders, taken away and put in a
proper beehive and brought back again. A huge bill arrived with

this rather rickety beehive, and the bees - who promptly went and died! Having paid £600 to have them taken away and then brought back, they might have had the grace to live for a bit! That was a sign the house needed something doing to it. Also some of the chimneys were leaning at an alarming angle and had quite a lot of flora and fauna growing out of them. We used to have an invasion, annually, of Jackdaws coming down the chimneys. The Jackdaws were rather surprised when we had this chimney lined and instead of gently fluttering down they came down a bit like it was a Helter Skelter. They'd come crashing down, lie rather stunned at the bottom, then start their flight round the room making a terrible mess of the bookcases.

Justin Coldwell b.1953

And the Perks family were happily shoehorned into a tiny cottage in Annscroft:

It was down the bottom end of Annscroft, a two-bedroomed cottage right opposite the church. If you go there now they've knocked the cottage down and built a garage - which is not much smaller than the cottage was! It was wonderful. We were rough, we were tough - I was running around with the backside out of my trousers. Dad was quite strict, but he was kind. There were eleven of us there. It was 1938 when we moved to Kennel lane. Eleven children and two grownups living in a two-bedroomed cottage. There were three beds in one room and we couldn't move around the beds. I slept with me brother. We used to get into a very cold bed - icicles on the windows, no bathroom, toilet up the garden. We made do.

Gordon Perks b.1929

Up in the Clee:

The first house was a brick house. It had got a wash house or a brewhouse where we did the washing and brewed the beer and that was held up by the outside toilet. If the outside toilet fell down - down would come the brewhouse! In the winter you put on your top coat, your hat and a muffler round your neck to go down to the loo.

Dennis Crowther b.1926

Ivy Bebb's house had a rather eccentric water supply:

Our water supply was always very erratic, then they put an electric motor in and you didn't have to pump it, you could go and turn a tap in the bakehouse. You'd take your bucket out.

26

27

Then they went onto the water supply that was for Hardwicke Estate, that supplied most of the village and we actually had a tap in the house. When they had the Foot and Mouth disease epidemic here they stopped keeping cows at Pool House farm and the water stopped, because the water pipe used to go through the cow house and when the cows had gone it froze!

Ivy Bebb b.1930

And sometimes the lights were a little haphazard, too:

When we got electricity we had two lights downstairs and two upstairs and money in the meter, so if you were halfway upstairs and the lights went out you'd got to come down in the dark and put the money in.

Annie Bebb b.1905

Ivor Southorn's brother was a little confused by the arrival of electricity in Broseley:

It was in 1932 that they built the power station at Buildwas and that's why we got power. We didn't get our first wall socket till after the war because I can remember when my mother got an electric iron she plugged it into a double socket stuck into the light fitting up above. But one time my brother and I were playing "Hide the Thimble" and I had to wait outside the kitchen whilst he tried to hide this metal thimble. But there were that many holes in the kitchen door where locks had been and keyholes had been cut I remember looking though a hole and seeing him look up at this two way socket ... and I thought, "Oh! That's where he's going to hide it!". The next thing I saw him get onto the table ... and of course he pushed this thimble up into the socket, which was live. It burnt two holes in the thimble, blew all the lights in the Kings Head and we got a damn good hiding too. But it's a wonder he's in one piece. We've still got the thimble here somewhere. It's a metal thimble with one hole going straight through and one partly through. And that was the end of the 'Hiding the Thimble' game.

So you and your brother didn't understand how electricity worked?
No we didn't! Mind you people don't understand it now. We had a girl in the hotel yesterday morning with a piece of bread stuck in the electric toaster and she was sticking the bread knife down it to clear it out!

Ivor Southorn b.1925

And a vivid description of the facilities from Emily Griffiths:

The You-Know-What was down the bottom of the garden and
it was my job every week to scrub it. I was doing that before
I was seven. And it was my job also to cut nice sized pieces of
newspaper and hang them on string behind the door. And if we
had new dresses wrapped in tissue paper, then the tissue paper
was ironed and cut into squares and put in a box on the seat
for the use of visitors. And my sister next to me used to annoy
me inexpressibly because she wouldn't use the newspaper; she
always insisted on using the visitors' pieces. We also had a box
of soil kept on the seat with a little bit of quicklime in it and
once the toilet had been used it was the duty to take the little
shovel and sprinkle a little quick lime and soil into the toilet;
which would be emptied once a year under the plum trees
in the garden and then we had plums like nobody's business.
Or should I say "everybody's business". I've got an outside
loo now because my second husband wouldn't tolerate an
inside one.

Emily Griffiths b.1917

**We had a washing machine long before anybody else.
I was showing it off proudly to my elderly Aunt one
day and she said, "It's marvellous, marvellous!
Now tell me, do you wash your clothes before you
put them in?"**

Meredith Lamont b.1915

*Washing, ironing, mending - all done without the labour
saving devices we have today:*

I don't iron a thing now. Nothing at all, do I iron. Not even
blouses. They go in the tumble drier after I've washed them
and if you don't put many in, you're alright. But in the old days
you ironed all day long sometimes when you washed for people.
An iron hotted on the fire. I never had electric irons till after the
electric came in, in 1956. People would ask you to do a day's
washing for them. Other cottagers, better off than us perhaps.
And sometimes you washed at home and sometimes you washed
at their place. I used to sew a lot too. When I was at school
I used to make the school teacher's undergarments. That was
hard work. I used to make her slips all by hand - backstitch and
the lot.

Molly Rowson b.1908

Muriel Painter and her brother Colin Brown, described the now demolished Phoenix Place in Mardol, Shrewsbury:

I was born in Phoenix Place in Mardol which was a terrible old slum area. My mother and father moving from Phoenix place to Coton Hill must have been like moving to heaven. The house at Phoenix Place was rented - well it wasn't a house, more like an old shack really with an earthenware floor, One down and one up ... The walls between each house were cardboard. My uncle would tell you that when one or two came in on a Saturday night when they were drunk and fighting an arm would come through the wall! ... There were only two or three toilets for this whole lot - and no lock on the door. He [my uncle] always used to sing when he went down there. There was no water as such - there was a standpipe and also another sort of shack thing with a great boiler and the council used to bring the hot water down on a Monday for them to wash ... all of them used to wash in there [the clothes]. The night soil man used to come and take the sewerage from the toilets and used to tip it into the river at Frankwell just the other side of the Welsh bridge ... [the front door] was small ... my mother and father had to bend down to get into it. It was as dark as could be. There was a range there. Then you seemed to go up two or three steps and there would be one bedroom, curtained off into different sections. My family moved in 1925 but my cousins stayed there another ten years.

Muriel Painter b.1925 and Colin Brown b.1931

All a little different from the house David Lloyd moved into in Ludlow:

My parent's greatest joy was to buy their own home in the 1950s. Both families came from the sort of background where you rented accommodation. They had modest but respectable houses and when my parents got married just before the second world war when unemployment still stalked the land their vision was to get their own house. They saved hard for it throughout the war, and after the war - when saving was respectable and much encouraged. When I was eighteen they were able to buy a very nice house on the edge of Ludlow. This was the triumph of my father's life. He was a man of modest tastes and immensely proud of his house and his garden. He bought a plot of land and commissioned a local builder to build it for him. They got enormous pleasure helping to design it and saying what they wanted. They had a small mortgage which my mother, as a teacher, was able to attain, but most of it was paid for by money saved.

Can you describe this house? In the design of it, what were they looking for?

A nice kitchen. My mother had grown up in a small part of an old Georgian vicarage in Newtown and the kitchen was meagre. So one of her ambitions was a nice kitchen with surfaces and cupboards and a Rayburn, the sort of thing we all take for granted today. Then we had a large lounge for entertaining and a separate dining room, which was regarded as a bit of a luxury, and a separate toilet and bathroom which was also considered very desirable. But the thing they liked best about the house was the view. The house was situated on the Sheet road and had a wonderful view over Ludlow... You could see the Castle and the Whitcliffe and the church. It was certainly regarded as a status symbol and they were very proud of it. Ludlow tradesmen had been moving out of town to large Victorian villas in Gravel Hill since the 19th Century and what happened to my parents was the tail end of that process.

David Lloyd b.1935

Ludlow also had its share of poverty:

Many people in Ludlow quite frankly lived in appalling conditions and I was made very much aware of this when I used to go round delivering groceries as a boy. My impression is that the poverty levels were as bad as they were in some of the big cities between the wars, but not on the same scale. We're talking about a few hundred families, perhaps, rather than thousands of families. But I can remember people coming to the British School at the beginning of the War and the teachers being concerned about the way they were clothed and shod. And if you went into many of the Ludlow slums you'd find paper partitions dividing boys and girls in one bedroom. People all crowded in together in one heated room. Very poor plumbing. A good deal of the poorer housing in Ludlow was very bad indeed.

David Lloyd b.1935

Were people keen to be moved out [during the Shrewsbury slum clearances]?

I think they were. It smelt terrible in Barker Street with that tannery. You could smell it for miles ... and those little tiny houses ... I know my sister-in-law's family lived in one of them and you'd see these people ... they'd be sitting outdoors rather than be in the house ... even into the winter ... they were terrible, they were so small and they were bug ridden too.

Muriel Painter b. 1925 and Colin Brown b. 1931

A last word from Telford:

It was exciting to arrive in Telford. Everything looked beautiful and fantastic and until I settled down it was just like a holiday. We had a lot of information about Europe so we knew what life was like. My husband had already rented a house in Randlay. The house is very huge for me. Japanese houses are described as rabbits' houses. So how could I live in such a huge house with only my husband ? It's a detached house with four bedrooms. We don't have many brick houses in Japan ... so it looks very pretty. But some things are very strange for me. The way you have a bath is different. In Japan we have a waterproof room with a bath tub and a washing area. We wash our hair and body with soap in the washing area and then rinse ourselves before climbing in the bath tub. So the bath water is always clear and we don't need to change it from person to person. But the English bathroom is different and we wondered how to use it without getting soap in the bath water. It's very strange for us. The house has a big garden which we don't have in Japan. It's very hard work and Japanese people are not very good at gardening, so I let my husband mow the lawn. I could say it's just a toilet for my dog!

Noaki Midori b. 1965

CHAPTER 3

WHO ARE WE?

Migration, emigration, immigration - these were the topics that came up in this section. Is there still a "Proud Salopian"? We talked to the people who were born and bred here and the people who have moved here and now consider Shropshire to be their home. We talked to people who live here but still consider their heart belongs in another place. We discovered stories from people who only found out who they were by chance. Some who discovered a family they never knew existed and some who never wanted to find their natural parents. There are stories from the transient population of Japanese people who work in Telford and from the Jamaicans who made their homes here in the 1950s. Does where we live make us who we are? Or is it the heritage we bring with us, or being able to trace the roots of our family back through generations?

An only child born with a tremendous link with the county of his birth Jon Hayward felt the history of the county through his family:

My great, great, great, great, great grandfather drove the coach from the Lion in Shrewsbury to London. Sam Hayward - he was listed in the book of Shropshire eccentrics.

I spent a lot of time as a youngster with my grandparents - a lot of the stories my grandfather told me were stories his grandfather had told him and he was born in 1815.

Jon Hayward b.1951

My mother was brought up in Greenfields (Shrewsbury). My grandfather became what was known as the Top Link Guard on the LMS and as a child I can remember the gorgeous braid he used to have on his cap - a very important man. Greenfields was the residential area of the upper echelon of the railway - because the railway was Shrewsbury. It was a station used jointly by the LMS and the GWR. Castlefields, where my father was brought up, would probably be looked on today as the slums of Shrewsbury. I was brought up in a sort of mixed marriage. From my mother, the Greenfields side, came the ambition to raise the status. I sometimes wonder how the deuce my mother and father got together and got married!

Gordon Riley b.1922

My father was an annealer, the thing that I remember most was the smell of his clothes when he came home, which always smelt hot and chemically. He was working in Tube Industries in Oldbury. I think as a result of finding out about what he did I became interested in industrial geography and particularly in people's places of work.

Jo Havell b.1943

Oswestry born Mary Hignett began to experience that feeling of being "different":

The National School was not very demanding or exciting but I won a scholarship at ten to go to the High School and that was a real eye-opener ... my sister started it. She said, "I'm going for the scholarship", and the girl who was with us was horrified. She said, "If you go to the High School you darsen't eat butties in the street".

Mary Hignett b.1912

Extended families where much more common:

We all lived together, you see, Grandfather and Grandmother, Mum and Dad, my brother and me. They were my mother's parents. I talked more with my grandfather. He wasn't grammar school educated but he was a very knowledgeable man, taught me about the world around me, the names of the trees. He'd take me into the Mogg forest and tell me about the ancient Britons.

Joyce Bunce b.1921

I can see my father's eyes in both of my sons.
Bill Caddick b.1944

Ruth Walmsley's family give her her sense of who she is:

My father was a very interesting man. He was an importer and exporter to begin with, of ivories, furs and antiques, then he was a furrier, and then he had his own carpet business ... He was born in Russia in 1888 and died when he was 84. He fled from the revolution. He was in Latvia and was Jewish. All his family fled really - his brothers, they got the first boat out so they didn't even know where they were going to land. One of his brothers landed in America, and two landed here. He landed in Swansea. He was brought up with a very minimal education but he was a very intelligent self-educated man. He grew up an atheist - he sort of turned his back on religion (not on being Jewish - he was always very proud of being Jewish). But then he met his wife and they talked about if there could be such a thing as an afterlife and they said, "Whichever one of us goes first, lets try and prove it to the other".

Ruth Walmsley b.1943

*Jon Hayward discovered his love of music was inherited
from his family:*

> When I was a small boy in the farmhouse I found my great
> great, great uncle's violin and all his music that had been written
> out in 1852. The originals of those are now in the museum at
> Ironbridge and I've got copies of them still. The fiddle had gone
> too far to be restored. There wasn't music in the immediate
> family - my mother sung but didn't play an instrument - nobody
> but my grandfather's sister who played mandolin. I decided
> when I was ten that I wanted to, so I arranged lessons down at
> Ludlow Grammar School, and good old Miss Verden who was
> the peripatetic violin teacher came in every week and gave me
> a lesson. I just like that instrument. I did try the trumpet but
> I couldn't get a very attractive sound from it. I played a little bit
> for South Shropshire Morris and then subsequently went to folk
> clubs in the area and sang and played there. I'd played for the
> rapper dance team when I was at university. Our idea of a good
> night is to go down to a local pub with some friends and take
> over a pub for an evening, sing and play and get everyone
> involved. I'm teaching myself button accordion at the moment
> and trying to learn the piano accordion as an alternative.
>
> **Jon Hayward b.1951**

> My father was a Freemason, a quite enthusiastic Freemason.
> When he died the Craft stepped in, as they do with anybody
> who's parents have died, to educate the sons and daughters
> who were left, either in their own schools or in other public
> schools. I could have gone to Oswestry, Ludlow or Shrewsbury
> but I was sent to London. I wasn't consulted about it. In those
> days you didn't consult a child of eight about things like that.
>
> **Brian Barrett b.1929**

*An accident nearly put paid to Terry Lowe arriving in this
world at all:*

> My mother came from quite a large family and her mother
> died tragically aborting twins - she haemorrhaged and died quite
> young from loss of blood in 1938. My mother, as the oldest girl,
> took charge at the age of fifteen and did it well. She got a job at
> Shrewsbury railway station as a trolley girl for the refreshments.
> On a quiet Sunday afternoon about three o'clock she apparently
> climbed out of the window at the front of the railway station
> and onto the glass veranda over the forecourt. They say that
> she was looking for a kitten that had strayed out onto the glass.
> All of a sudden, the glass gave way and she fell quite a way

35

down onto the pavement. Some passers-by came across what they thought was her body. She had very serious head injuries, a couple of fractures, and she was unconscious in hospital for about three days. When I was doing family research I went to Shrewsbury Records and Research Centre and I looked up the newspapers because I was anxious to find out all I could about this. I knew roughly the date but when I came across the headline "Girl falls through glass roof" it was a strange feeling to read about the woman who was to become my mother. It was touch and go at one stage, and if it hadn't been for a benefactor, the Mayor of Shrewsbury at the time, who paid for her convalescence at Llandudno, I think she could well have died and I may not be talking to you now. I've been there many times and stood in front of the station and thought, "This is where she fell. It could have all ended here on this pavement and I would never have had any grandchildren".

Terry Lowe b.1943

There are still times and places where you can meet with the true locals:

If you go into Madeley Churchyard around Christmas Eve it's like a reunion of the old Madeley people - we meet up with that many and we all laugh and say we should bring a flask and have a party. They all go to the churchyard on Christmas eve to tend the graves, they take a holly wreath - they don't knowingly gather but they go.

Della Bailey b.1928

There are such things as class differences too:

The only thing that matters is what you are. I will agree there are times when people marry into very different social backgrounds which can be a little aggravating. I had a friend who did that. She was a clergyman's daughter and she married a hairdresser from London and it didn't work at all really. He was quite happy to have the jam pot on the table and the butter in the paper and of course she hadn't been used to that. I concede you've got to be very sure it will work and you've got to be very fond of each other.

Vera Smith b.1916

My father got me into politics. But I got myself into being a politician.

Iris Butler b.1919

Liz Lawrence felt excluded in a different way:

Throughout the whole time that I've been in the army, I've not broadcast the fact because of the terrorist threat. So I've never once travelled to Shropshire in my uniform, ever. It was very rare that you'd actually tell anybody what you did, and that's quite sad.

It's a shame because you were proud of what you did.
Of course I was.

So did you feel marked out from society as a whole, socially?
Yes, because in the armed forces we have been 'not going out' for the last 25 years. We haven't been having parties in pubs. We've had to keep ourselves separate from the civilian population because you don't know who the civilian population are.

Regimental Sergeant Major Liz Lawrence b. 1955

People are slightly prejudiced against me 'cos I dress differently and listen to different music to most people. I get abuse, occasionally, which is a bit strange. I'm into glitter and feather and furs and things like that.

You mean, the 70s Glam-rock look?
Yes, that's it. I do it at college as well and sometimes I get the odd comment but it doesn't bother me. I'd like to have lived in the 70s when Glam-rock was king.

Miranda Richer b. 1983

Does the sense of place make us who were are?

In Bishop's Castle people are fulfilled in their own character and they don't try to perform, perhaps, to outside influences too much. There's a confidence in the local identity and integrity which allows people to be themselves more.

Robert Tomlinson b. 1957

St John's Hill was the Harley Street of Shrewsbury. It was where all the doctors lived. My father felt very strongly that he had to maintain a certain image. I think doctors in those days did. He had to have an expensive car and a brass plate that was well and truly rubbed down; it mustn't look too new. The great thing was to rub your name almost off, so it looked as though you had been there for many years. His consulting room here in the house was designed to impress. He took great care about this ... which was very interesting to me being brought up in a completely different way of thinking with the NHS coming in when I was eighteen.

Dr Patrick Anderson b.1930

Emma Bullock was nurse to Sir Jasper and Lady Moore at Linley Hall, near Bishops Castle. She was 'part of the family':

I was working for Lady Moore right into my eighties ... I lived with them as an equal. When I first knew Lady Moore at Linley Hall she had a full staff and a butler, but they all went off during the war and didn't come back.

Emma Bullock b.1911

Evelyn Hatton's links with the county have made her a true Salopian:

I was born in Wolverhampton but I like to think I'm a Shropshire girl. I suppose I'm a bit of both. I'd say yes I am a Salopian. I've lived here for 67 years and all my dad's family have lived here for generations ... I always thought of myself as a country girl, or as I like to put it, a ruddy country wench.

Evelyn Hatton b. 1926

It is difficult to become, or even work out who you are when you feel you don't fit the norm:

Thatcher's Britain didn't seem to have room for people like me. I didn't know where I fitted in. The thing at the time was Yuppies and money, and making money. It was totally beyond my ken.

Katherine Soutar b. 1963

There can be some identity stuff that can get a young gay man down. Because we don't have the wealth of foundation that everybody else does, means we're working very much in a vacuum. In a way we're bridging that, but we've come from a world where there were no models for us.

Geoff Hardy b. 1950

> The need for counselling has grown. We've always to some extent had counsellors, in extended families we went to people within the family, we always had an outsider, often a priest where you can unburden yourself. But what has happened is a questioning of the pillars that defined you. They've fallen. Without a structure - who are you?
>
> **Geoff Hardy b. 1950**

Madeley born Della Bailey talked about her sister's quest to better herself:

My sister emigrated. She was the most keen to get on ... she wanted to go to new horizons ... her boyfriend went to Australia and they were going to get married ... there was a big fuss. My mum and dad were very clinging and didn't want her to break up the family. She was a £10 migrant - they were bitter about it. Her first husband, the boyfriend, was only 42 when he died. She married again. She married very well - he was Acting Solicitor General. When she came home to visit with two children and her first husband the reunion was shunned. Dad went out to the chicken shed. They resented my sister's need to go away and better herself. They felt she should be content with her lot, that she shouldn't reach for the stars.

Della Bailey b. 1928

Of course everyone knows where we come from by the accent, or do they?

I went in the merchant navy and mixing with lads from Liverpool, Londoners, Geordies, suchlike. Of course the first thing they'd do was take the Mickey out of my Shropshire accent. "Ooo aaarr" they'd say. I thought, "Well, I'm going to have to change to stop them taking the Mick" - but I went worse really. Blow me, why should I change? A lot of folks would say, "are you from Wales?", and in the finish I'd say, "Well that's near enough". The interesting thing was one chap, and he was Northern Irish, Paddy he was. I hadn't been on the ship very long and he said, "do you come from Wexford?" I said "Where?" He said, "I'm sure by your accent you come from Wexford". That's the first time anyone thought I was Irish!

Terry Tandler b.1951

Most of my army friends ask where my accent's from. Oswestry has a very particular dialect and the person you hear with the best one is Ian Woosnam who's never lost his Oswestry accent. They tell me mine's the same.

Do people know where you're talking about when you say you're from Oswestry?

You do have to explain. It's got worse because twenty years ago when you said you were from Oswestry, they'd say, "Oh, that's where the Foot and Mouth was." People in the army sometimes know where it is because of Park Hall Camp, especially if they're Artillery.

Regimental Sargent Major Liz Lawrence b.1955

Born and brought up in the North-east, Squirrel spent time in Holland and is now living in Shropshire. He was initially curious about his roots:

When I was nine I asked my mum who my father was and she said, "you're not old enough". I asked her again when I was thirteen and she wouldn't answer. It wasn't until I was eighteen - it was a horrible situation. We were both crying and she told me his name and a little bit about him. Not much. When I was thirteen an uncle came and stayed in the North-east. He was from the Midlands and I asked him. I could talk to him differently from the rest of my family and he said, "Oh he's a bad man", but he didn't really know. I said this to my mum and she said, "No, he was just an ordinary bloke, nothing untoward about him". So I got his name and where he lived - where he did live - but that's about all. I don't think I need to meet him. I'm too much my own person. I don't want to go up to some man in their 60s or 70s and say, "Hello, I'm your son". He probably knows anyway. He did the business after all.

Squirrel b.1951

The last part of this chapter is devoted to someone who found out who she was by a chance remark in an interview with Dr Patrick Anderson.

Interestingly, around the night I was born at 23, St John's Hill in 1930, a baby girl was wrapped up and left on the doorstep by somebody who must have thought, "I can't afford to look after it, perhaps someone in St John's Hill will." They must have known this was a doctor's house and that doctors were thought to be sufficiently well endowed to look after an extra baby. So my mother had to cope with two of us.

What happened to your doorstep sister?
Well, I'm not sure. There's every reason to believe the baby lived and was brought up by somebody, but the details are lost I'm afraid. I simply don't know.

Dr Patrick Anderson b.1930

It was a slim chance that she still lived in the area and an appeal on BBC Radio Shropshire bought dividends when a man called in at the station and said he believed we were looking for his cousin.

Jean Baugh takes up her own story:

My parents never told me about my real origins. I was brought up by George Davis and his wife in Reabrook Avenue (Shrewsbury). I came across a newspaper cutting in my baby book. I was about ten. I don't know why I didn't ask. I didn't when I was older.

People have asked me didn't I want to know my real mother? But I said "no, if she didn't want me at least she left me some good parents." The baby book had little envelopes in it, first lock of hair - all sorts of things and the newspaper cutting was in it.

The cutting said you where found at a doctors but not who the doctor was.

When I found out who the doctor was I remembered my cousins' mum had worked for Dr Anderson and my dad's first wife couldn't have any family so I think that's how I came to be with them. My adopted Dad's sister worked for Dr Anderson - I think they'd been wanting someone to have me so perhaps she told them that my foster father and mother would be suitable. Then it had to go through the court to get me adopted... My real parents sound like they were rogues, itinerants. They gave up a son, too.

Jean Baugh b.1930

Jean Baugh's real parents were sentenced to three months hard labour for abandoning Jean and a three year old boy in Chester Market. They originally came from Chester.

Alas there is no firm conclusion to this story. Efforts are still being made to trace Jean's brother.

CHAPTER 4

BELONGING

What does it mean to belong and who belongs in Shropshire?
There are stories from the black community and comments
from the Welsh, the Japanese and the Chinese population.
They all have their tales to tell about their lives in
Shropshire.

I've given birth to four children in this country. I belong here
in Hadley. Since my husband died eighteen years ago ... and with
all my children here ... I feel I cannot go back to Jamaica to live,
and leave my children here - and be happy. My heart would
be here. My husband's buried across at the cemetery and
there is a place for me there when I go. If I go to Jamaica
now and die there, all my children and grandchildren could
not afford to go to my funeral. But if I die here, I know all
of them will be there.

Having said all that, when the West Indies come to play
cricket in England, who do you cheer for?

The West Indies, of course!

Ivy Gilpin b. 1928

When I first came here no coloured person was able to get
a council house. It was a blessing in disguise really because we
were determined to buy our own houses and it's worked out
for us.

Eulin Drummond b. 1936

Leon Murray received a warm welcome when he arrived:

When I arrived from Jamaica I got a taxi and said, "I've just
come from Jamaica and I want to catch a train to Wellington
in Shropshire". The driver parked his taxi, took my suitcase,
walked me to the station at Euston and saw I got the tickets
(£1 10/-). He walked me onto the platform and said to the
guard, "This young man is going to Wellington in Shropshire,
will you put him with somebody who is going that distance?"

but not quite so warm in Shropshire:

I remember walking down New Street in Wellington and
people moving to the other side of the street, but over time
people have come to accept me.

Leon Murray b. 1938

When we moved here we were the first black family in the street. Nobody spoke - you felt awful. The adjoining house was put up for sale two weeks later and a black man bought it. Then they all put up 'for sale' signs. It made me feel really sad. Why do people behave like this? We didn't molest them - we did nothing to upset them. It was just the colour of our skin. I bought this house in 1964. There are only two white people still here that were here when we came. All the rest said they didn't want to live among coloured people.

Eulin Drummond b. 1936

Jo Havell experienced prejudice on her return from Australia:

I think that I had more prejudice when I arrived back from Australia and went to secondary school, because of my accent, which I soon learnt to modify and also because I was very dark. I had thick curly black hair and a dark complexion because I'd been exposed to the great outdoor life. To a certain degree I experienced what it must have been like to be a black immigrant in this country. I think that gave me lessons for my life in how I've treated people. I remember the names I was called - "Nigger" and "Blackie" even though I was white. "Go back to your own country" which I found very difficult to explain. The fact that I felt the cold was put down to my 'different blood'. A whole range of things ... the anger about that has left me, but the sadness about the ignorance shown is still very strong.

Jo Havell b. 1943

There are a lot of white people in our area now because the black people bought the houses and they rent them out to the white. So what goes around comes around, and now we all get on very well together.

Eulin Drummond b. 1936

I was the first Afro-Caribbean Magistrate, perhaps in the Midlands. This July coming, it will be sixteen years that I have been on the Bench.

Leon Murray b. 1938

We had to learn the English ways. If you bought a TV, fridge or washing machine they had no plug. So you had to assemble it for yourself. I couldn't believe it. Why is there no plug? And one day I went back home to find a neighbour repairing his car. Amazingly, he was removing the engine from the car in his own drive.

Toshiro Shitara b. 1949

I came to England ten years ago when my daughter Rosie was only eight, and we've been in Wellington four years now.

So does your daughter feel she is English or Taiwanese?

That's a very interesting question because up to the age of fourteen she thought she was English. And most of the time she felt embarrassed by our attitude or manner. For example, when we Chinese go for a meal all together normally we fight between us for the honour of paying the restaurant bill. When she was young she didn't want to go to the restaurant with us because she'd say we were always arguing with each other. It embarrassed her. But now she's eighteen she's proud of her origin. She feels lucky because she is living between two cultures.

Xiaoying Tseng b. 1951

I married my first husband, John, in Jamaica when I was eighteen, and my first daughter Mavis is from him. He was a deacon at the Baptist Church and I sang in the choir. We had a wonderful white wedding. We ate goat, had a three-tier wedding cake and lots of reggae music - but no honeymoon. We couldn't afford it.

What made John want to come to England ?

Well, he had a good friend who was coming to England and he suggested they both went. John talked it over with me, but the bad part of it was that I was pregnant with Mavis. But I said, "You go. My mummy's here to help me. I'll be alright". So he came to England. He wanted a proper job. He was an educated man. But he couldn't get a good job in a bank in Jamaica and he didn't want to work on a farm.

What made him think that Britain would be better?

Well, a few lads from our parish came over before him and they wrote back to say, "You can work here and earn some money". It was a big decision. But after he came and got a job and got the first wage packet here, he took sick. He came here in March 1955 and he died in the August, before the baby was born. He's buried at Wolverhampton. So I didn't follow him. But a year later I decided to leave my baby with my mum to come to Britain to see where he was buried and to give him a tomb. I didn't come to stay, but when I got here a relative suggested I got a job to make some money. "Why pay all that money to come here", he said. "Get a job and earn back that money before you go home". So I wrote to my mum and she said "Your child is alright. If you want to stay a couple more months, you can." So I got a job at Eveready doing those batteries in Wolverhampton where I met my second husband,

Egbert, who I already knew from Jamaica. About twelve months later we got married. He was working at GKN Sankey so we moved from Wolverhampton to the new houses near the factory (in what was to become Telford). When I first came to Wolverhampton I didn't see much prejudice. There were more black people in Wolverhampton before I came, so they'd got used to us. But there were no black people in Telford when I came here. So I experienced a really rough time. If I went to Wellington on the bus and sat beside an English person, some of them would get up and move away. I had to say to them, "I'm the same person as you, only I've got black skin and you've got white skin. We're two races of people both created by God. Therefore I'm not going to hurt you". I'd say that out loud and they'd be embarrassed. They'd go redder ... and I'd go blacker!

Ivy Gilpin b. 1928

When I had my interview to be a magistrate one of the questions was very stupid. They asked me, "Mr Murray, if you were a magistrate and a black person came before you how would you adjudicate?" That tells me they imagined a person's colour and customs have a great effect on the judicial decisions they make - which it shouldn't.

Leon Murray b. 1938

Vicky Cowell was born in Jamaica and moved to Shropshire in the 1950s

I feel I belong here. I finally got citizenship. People who came here after Jamaica got independence are not British subjects. But I was a British subject because the English were ruling Jamaica at the time. I love the place and I like the people. I worked thirty-one and a half years at Sankeys. I worked with mostly English people and I never found any fault with them. I like them, we get on all right. You may find a few English people might be not much for black people, but I don't take any notice of them.

Vicky Cowell b. 1931

When I was promoted to inspector in 1983 and put in charge of community relations, I knew a policeman who every time he shook hands with a black or Asian man used to go and wash his hands. I'd say, "What are you doing that for?" And he'd say, "Well, you never know what they've got".

Terry Lowe b. 1943

47

Although the troubled times of the Welsh versus the English in Shrewsbury have gone, Gareth Jenkins maintains his nationality:

I will always feel Welsh. I will feel Welsh and I'll feel British, but I'll never be English. So I have to live the life slightly of an exile even though I still feel I'm in my country. I came to live in Shrewsbury because it's just further down the River Severn for me. I was born in the upper reaches of The Severn and as you go down the river the towns get slightly bigger - from Llanidloes to Newtown to Welshpool to Shrewsbury. Shrewsbury was the place where, as a child, we would go if we had any serious economic things to do. Historically of course Shrewsbury became one of the wealthiest towns in England by virtue of its position in relation to Wales and the Severn Valley. The wool producers of Wales did all their trading in Shrewsbury. So Shrewsbury is an integral part of Mid-Wales life. We have our hospital here. There's a huge Welsh population in Shrewsbury itself. At the Flower Show it's wonderful to hear the Welsh National Anthem played alongside "God Save the Queen". Nobody raises any objection to that, so I don't feel that Shrewsbury is fully English. It is a border town, and that's why I feel at home here. My father advised me when I wanted to find a place to work as a dentist, "Go to Shrewsbury."

Would you ever live any further east?
No, I wouldn't. In fact I still want to live on the west side of Shrewsbury. I want to look out to Wales.

Gareth Jenkins b. 1956

CHAPTER 5

LIVING TOGETHER

Sex comes under the close scrutiny of Shropshire people in this chapter, together with morality, divorce, the extended family and gay relationships. How our concepts have altered over the century. There is talk of courting in Shrewsbury in the early part of the century, vows of celibacy, divorce and microwaves, and a look at sex education before World War Two.

Former Vicar of Myddle, John Ayling, describes how he met the lady who was to become his wife:

> We met by accident - when I was first entering into the church I was rather high church. I thought a priest ought to be celibate and give his whole time to the service of his church and his people. That was my settled conviction and I held women at arms length though I loved them all. I never had tea at home because all the mothers with eligible daughters always invited me to tea and told me what wonderful people their daughters were, and what wonderful cooks. I didn't want anything to do with them. Then I met Winifred. She always sat at the church right at the back. I didn't even notice her. Her half nephew had an accident and we thought he'd loose his sight. I used to visit him in the hospital and when he went home I called on him. She opened door to me. She thought I was the man bringing the groceries. She said, "put them on the step and I'll take them in, in a minute". I said, "No I'm the parson. I've come to visit your nephew." By the next week I'd fallen for her. After that all my vows of celibacy went by the wind. I met her at Easter and we were married that September. She had a like mind. We got engaged. I gave her a ring with three diamonds. It cost all I'd got. Two diamonds were quite small with a quite large one in the middle. I said, "This is the pattern of our lives. Those two small diamonds, that's you and me. The big diamond is Our Lord. The gold band is the love to bind us all together. So if our life is to be what I want it to be: you and I, Our Lord always at the centre, and our love binding us all together." That's how we tried to live and to teach our children.

The Reverend John Ayling b. 1902

Gordon Rose's courting days were less orthodox:

> I went to Birmingham university as a medical student where I met my wife. Our early courting days were done in the

dissecting room. She was in the year below me. I made her acquaintance at the weekly hop which was for learning about the other sex. It was my first acquaintance with them! We got better acquainted taking the human body to pieces.

Gordon Rose OBE b.1916

Eamon Daly has pinned his hopes on his three year old son to put him on the straight and narrow:

I've never really bothered before but now I think it's time to stop thieving, knock crime on the head and get a job. I've got a son out there who's gone three. I've only known him for six months of his life. The rest of the time I've spent in prison. It's not fair on him and it's not fair on my girlfriend, who I'm still with now - believe it or not after all these years. She's stood by me and I've just got another three year sentences. All in all I've had a ten and a half year prison sentence with all my sentences put together. I'm 23. I've spent nearly seven years in prison all in all.

Eamon Daly b. 1975

How did you get a date with Kathleen?

There was a little sweetshop at number 9, Castle Foregate. Two ladies kept it. I used to leave a note there for her and she used to leave a note there for me.

Edgar Gibbs b. 1908

It seemed courting was quite difficult in the early part of the century:

About the only time we ever saw each other was after church on a Sunday, when we used to go for a walk hoping none of the Parish would recognise us. That was all we had. But it didn't matter; we were quite sure of ourselves. No question about it. Falling in love was a more official affair. There were very strong social barriers. I remember the Parish always linked me up with the doctor's daughter. I think he did too. A parson was somebody up there you see! Hanky panky didn't happen in those days much - well not in my book. There were opportunities when women would have welcomed my attentions - but I wouldn't have. I was always going to be a priest and priests didn't do that sort of thing. That's always been my salvation. We are more in love now than we were when we were first married. You know I write her poetry. It's been published. On our 65th wedding anniversary I wrote an Ode to Winifred and it was published with comments in the (Shrewsbury) Chronicle. We're still hopelessly in love with each other after 65 years and there's nothing she doesn't do for me.

The Reverend John Ayling b. 1902

Meredith Lamont discovered the way to the man's heart was through his stomach:

I met my husband-to-be in hospital. I was an American nurse and he was a wounded Scottish soldier. He'd lost a leg in Africa and for him the war was over. He would ask a favour and I would see if we could grant it. One of his visitors brought him two shell eggs and he said, "Would you cook these eggs for me?" I said, "Any fool can cook an egg". Now a shelled egg at that time was really something, and two was more wonderful still. So I fried the eggs very nicely. That morning on the menu were American flapjacks ... big pancakes with a ladle full of thin syrup poured over the top. So I put the eggs on a plate and I passed it to the sergeant who poured the syrup on. Well, when it got to Willy he turned a kind of greenish lavender and he wouldn't eat the eggs. Well, that was a blow to our relationship. And then later somebody brought him a haggis and, courageous as he was, he asked if I would cook it for him. I said, "I can cook eggs, but how do you cook a haggis?" "Well," he said, "I think you boil them". I used my own judgement. I got a big pan and filled it full of water so the haggis would be well immersed. And I waited until the little bubbles were on the bottom coming up. And then I peeled the haggis and put it in ... ! He married me after all that!

Meredith Lamont b. 1915

There was virtually no discussion about sex:

We never discussed sexual matters. In fact I came back from the continent when I was in the RAF and stayed at home a few nights before I was married. I remember my father saying, "I suppose I ought to give you a few words about 'life' now you are going to get married". I said, "I don't think you need bother Pop, I've learnt most of it" and he said, "Thank God for that!"

Gordon Riley b. 1922

When I was at Adams Grammar School in Newport you weren't allowed to talk to girls in the street and I was hauled into the headmaster's office one day. He said, "Dawbarn, I saw you talking to a girl in the street". I said, "That was my sister, sir." "That doesn't make any difference, Dawbarn!" Ridiculous isn't it, now.

Peter Dawbarn b. 1921

The nearest one got to sex in those days was when the girls went out on the playing field with their shirts tucked in their knickers playing netball or whatever. I don't even remember reading books on sex.

Gordon Riley b. 1922

If you were in the police force you had to be pretty sure of the girl you were to marry:

It was true of the police force that if you wanted to marry, your wife had to be vetted to prove her good character, until somebody sussed out in the 50s that no-one vetted the Chief Constable's wife - then it stopped. My wife was vetted, but I can't recall if she had to provide a reference. You had to inform your Superior, because it would alter the way you were dealt with in terms of housing. You could see the sense of it in some ways. If you married into a family where your relatives were regularly being prosecuted you could be open to inducements.

— Richard Blythe b. 1926

The freedom we know in the 1990s was certainly not approved of in the 20s and 30s:

Living together before marriage was almost unheard of and illegitimacy was a great shame - traumatic. So you tried not to let it happen. Nowadays that's gone. People like to go to church for a white wedding more for the show than the reality, though some take it seriously, thank God. The whole concept has changed.

The Reverend John Ayling b. 1902

Whatever you did to get babies only happened in the marriage bed and in any case dabbling with such things could bring terrible consequences. I never knew what those consequences were until the RAF Flight Sergeant explained the sort of things you didn't do.

Gordon Riley b. 1922

Or was it?

We were very ignorant about homosexuals. I didn't know what a homosexual was till I joined the Forces when I was eighteen. We knew about illegitimate children though. In my father's day the stallion used to come round to the local farms brought by a groom who'd stay the night. Then, nine months later there'd be an addition to the farmer's family. Or it might be the milkmaid. But it was more important for the mare to get pregnant than for the milkmaid not to.

Alf Cheadle b. 1922

There was also the things I didn't understand until later when
girls were closeted away because they'd got into trouble and
those were the people who hadn't stuck to the rules. The funny
thing is they never explained the rules at that early stage!

Gordon Riley b. 1922

*If you did need to find things out Fred Jordan suggested
the local smithy:*

Of course the blacksmith's shop was a meeting place for people
from all over. Chaps would come in with their horses and gossip
while they were waiting, all the gossip, like - nothing for your
ears. Who was expecting, or like to be expecting and who was
likely to be the father too.

There wasn't so much a stigma having a child out of marriage,
here like. Country folks took it like it was - the wench went on
working and the old folks looked after the kid, you see.
They were all sent for a purpose we used to say.

Fred Jordan b. 1922

When I think about it there was nobody young of our own
age from my village at the wedding. They were all away at war.
We were in love and we got married but we never lived
together as a couple until 1945. There must have been lots of
women whose husbands went away right at the beginning of
the war ... gone for five or six years. And when they came back
they must have been total strangers.

Cath Marshall b. 1920

*And the romantic notion of the wedding night didn't
always go smoothly:*

Sex never came into my life until we were married. I'd never
had any sexual experience with anybody because I knew it to
be wrong. The first experience of my honeymoon was so funny
- I could make a film of it. He'd got one day's leave from the
Air Force. I'd bought some beautiful undies and I'd shown them
to my sister and mother. When we got the hotel they were
single beds and no heating in the bedroom and it was freezing -
and there was me a virgin - my husband a virgin - but the first
thing he said was, "We've got to heat this bedroom up".

Well it was a gas fire and we didn't smoke so how were we going to get matches. There was a water heater in the bathroom - one with a gas jet - and he found a piece of paper and lit this - walked along the landing to light the gas fire. Then of course it didn't light because you had to put money in the slot.

Beryl Gower b. 1918

> **Premarital sex wasn't a thing that happened in the best circles.**
>
> **Gordon Riley b. 1922**

Not everyone was allowed the luxury of marriage:

People in a profession, if they got married, they immediately lost their jobs. Teachers, they weren't allowed to work if they were married. I remember when I was at college, some girls had their boyfriends, but the Principal always had to see this young man. She always told him what a wonderful teacher Miss so and so was and what a pity it would be if she didn't continue her profession ...

Is that why you never married?

Well, it was the war and it was our generation. So many young men got killed ...

Vera Smith b. 1916

Inmate from Shrewsbury Prison, Eamon Daly told a harrowing tale about his relationship with his girlfriend:

I've known my girlfriend for years, I met her through a friend in 1991. We were together on and off until 1993. She became pregnant in 1992 and I got locked up in '93 - I got five years. She gave birth in July 1993 and the baby died, which did my head in but I was locked up and there was nothing I could do.

Eamon Daly b.1975

Gordon Perks did his courting in the open air:

I met Margaret in Pontesbury. We used to do our courting on Pontesford Hill. We used to go in a gang courting. It's messy now, but it used to be lovely and I proposed up there. This was after I'd joined up with the navy. I remember coming home on leave and going to Margaret's father. I remember him saying to me, "You can court Margaret if you'll bring me a rabbit and a swede and a bag of potatoes out of the garden." It was a small price to get a lovely girl like Margaret.

Gordon Perks b. 1929

And Evelyn Hatton fell in love the second time around while she was in Church:

I've been playing the organ at Chapel for 56 years now. I played at Pontesbury for 50 years and when I came to Whittington my former Minister wrote to the Minister here and said "Ev plays the organ". So I've been playing at West Felton Chapel since 1992. My present husband Bert's daughter had a barn conversion house, and he moved to live here. He came to our chapel. He was widowed as well. I was 67 when I fell in love for the second time. It seems a funny thing to say at our ages, that we were falling in love but it was a lovely relationship. It sort of grows on you slowly. I met my first husband Tom when I was playing for the male voice choir at Pontesbury and he said "you smiled at me over the organ" - so I think it was the same both times.

Evelyn Hatton b. 1926 ———

As the century moved on there was a little more enlightened sex education:

Mother did prepare me for what was going to happen to me and if I reported what I'd learnt about the facts of life from elsewhere she'd reinforce or correct it. We had open conversations about it. She talked about it "not being wise to anticipate marriage" and "the risks of pregnancy". Yes, that was talked about but she used to say, "Don't mention it in front of your father!"

Cynthia Rickards b. 1937 ———

Looking back on the wedding day:

We married in 1948 I came home on leave and we were allowed to wear naval uniform. It was a red hot day in July. Pretty well all the village turned out - in Pontesbury. We had a good reception. The family put it on. Margaret was working then for her uncle who was the local grocer and I think he helped out quite a lot because everything was on ration. There was a big reception which was at the Deanery Hall. It's still there. It's opposite Hignetts. No honeymoon. You didn't have them in them days, but we've had many since! I only had about seven days leave.

Gordon Perks b. 1929

What kind of wedding did you have in 1941?
A very quiet one ... we got married at 9 o'clock at St Mary's Church [Shrewsbury]. There were eight people there. We went for the day to Liverpool and came back that night and I was in the Shrewsbury auction next morning, grading.

Edgar Gibbs b.1908

We got married at St Michael's, West Felton. We had a lovely day. The Morris dancers came to our wedding. They said to my daughter, "We'd love to come to your mum's wedding". She's in Five Speed Box the Ceilidh band, she plays concertina. The Morris dancers made a guard of honour and they danced afterwards on the road, in the wet. It was lovely. My son Malcolm Corfield gave me away and Bert's son Stephen Hatton was the best man.

Evelyn Hatton b. 1926

Or there is an alternative version to the wedding ceremony:

There's another way to get married - the gypsy way - where you both pee in a bucket, swirl the bucket round and say - right - you can't separate those waters - you can't separate these two people. There's a lot of ways of looking at a marriage.

Squirrel b. 1951

Work may mean happily married people need to live apart:

It isn't the nicest thing in the world every Sunday afternoon for me to climb into the car and say, "See you on Friday", but there are millions of people in this situation. It is an increasing pattern in this day and age because people are very reluctant to leave their homes. We've now got a home in Yorkshire which we like very much. We like the village, we like the area and all those things stack up to make the alternative, which is to move house, far less attractive. My wife has an extremely important job with Leeds University, and what's the difference between my job and hers? If she was transferred to another university, would I move house and leave my job behind? I have a weekend wife now and she has a weekend husband - and she may quite like that ! But I rent a flat in Shrewsbury and we do try to make the best of it. She visits me when she takes time off during the week and I'll go up to Yorkshire sometimes for a long weekend and tensions don't seem to have been created by the situation. We both know it's not for ever. There'll be another career development, another opportunity, another change.

Alan Bramley b. 1948

I've never bothered with marriage. I've never liked to be tied down. I've had women, like, but not one I'd like to marry. It would have been nice to have a son to sing my songs - I've given a good few a start but it's not the same.

Fred Jordan b. 1922

After marriage the children are almost inevitable:

I have eleven children, thirty-two grand children and forty-five great grand children. All my children are happily married and all live locally. The furthest away is the youngest at Bishop's Castle.

Why did you have so many children?

Well, we didn't take the precautions they take today. My husband liked a drink - I don't mean to say he got drunk. Every evening he liked to go out and have a pint and come back again before bedtime. And I used to say, "I must be bad company", and he used to say, "No it's not that, it's just a change". He said," I can talk to the men folk". Otherwise he was a footballer, really. He played for Pontesbury and then Snailbeach and Hope Valley. He used to rush home from the mines on a Saturday, just grab a sandwich or something, change and walk over to Hope Valley and have his game of football.

Of course his brothers were with him - and my brother - and very often I wouldn't see him till early Sunday morning because after the match all these lads together liked to go up to the dance and he had a drink of course. He used to keep saying, "Oh dear, I must go. I've left Nell on her own", but he didn't come home till they came home, like. But we were always happy and never fell out. I was at home bringing up the children. I felt it was my place anyway. I couldn't go out like some of these go out now. I think a married woman should be at home with the children.

How many years between the oldest and the youngest?

The oldest is 65 and the youngest 43.

So for 22 years you had a baby every other year?

Yes. Pretty well.

So you were either always pregnant or always nursing.

One or the other, yes. You wouldn't catch many women doing that now.

Did you discuss with your husband how many children you wanted to have?

No, we didn't discuss it at all. It just happened. Mind, he was a good father.

Would you have used the pill if it were available in your day?

Yes, I think I would. But then - look at what I would have missed.

Nellie Rowson b. 1914

Nothing in my lifetime has changed the social environment more than 'the pill'. It didn't just liberate women it gave them the opportunity to be selective and aggressive. I was on the council at the time. And I was on a governing body for a teacher training college and I wanted to put the pill into slot machines. I mean we always had two or three girls having to leave every year because they were pregnant. They were going out and experimenting in life and we weren't giving them the tools to protect themselves with. But I couldn't get a seconder for the motion. I couldn't even get a seconder for the motion to install a contraceptive machine either. Three generations later it's led to sex and love being completely separate issues. And a lot of widows in my generation who didn't have that adolescent freedom now want a taste of it, you know. They saw their daughters having the sexual freedom they never had and they want to try it a bit. They don't want to die with just one man under their belt.

Merrick Roocroft b. 1937

Divorce was a social stigma:

There were some drawbacks to being divorced. My sister and I used to say we were widows, because widows were more respected than divorcees. It was difficult socialising with your married friends - well you're spare aren't you? A lot of people I thought were my friends - when we divorced they preferred to be friends with my husband ... but I never wanted to get married again. I never will.

Della Bailey b. 1928

And could be difficult for children:

My mum asked if her new boyfriend could move into our house and he's been here ever since. But it's quite difficult because I'm almost scared he's gonna try and take over as a father and that's not what I want at all. I think I've got a phobia about step-parents 'cos my dad had a baby with this women I didn't really get on with. Well, I knew her really well before - but when she moved in she was rather horrible to me - so I have this phobia about step parents. She tried to act like a mother too much towards me and I didn't like that at all.

So what should a step-parent do?
I don't think they should interfere with the step-children.
They try and act as parents too early and I don't really like that.

Miranda Richer b. 1982

It is so important to keep an open mind because not all marriages are 'happy ever after':

I was avidly against divorce and then one of my friends married a divorcee and I remember saying to her, "I hope we can remain friends, but I'm afraid I can't go along with marrying divorcees".

I've since felt that was not the right thing to say. I've changed my mind mainly, I think, because I have interviewed so many people who've been divorced and are now marrying for a second time. I've heard some of the stories they have to tell. I've changed my mind completely because when people marry they think it's going to be for a lifetime, and they're quite sure of that when they make their promises. But something happens and it doesn't work out like that and having thought it through I feel that it's better for people to be divorced than live a life of misery attached to one person - like so many people did in Victorian times and before the war. They lived through hell. So surely it's better to be given a second chance and a better life by remarrying; having learned, hopefully, from the first marriage. Personally I interview people and go through a form of confession, sitting with the wife or husband-to-be of the second marriage, so that things of the first marriage are totally cleared out of the way. Perhaps even burn things that are still on their minds. I will remarry people now who have been divorced. And I think I began my rethinking in the sixties and it's taken forty years.

Rev. Ann Hadley b. 1933

I'd thought about leaving my husband very carefully but the timing had to be very precise. I had a car, and could carry out a microwave. I thought, "what can I put in the microwave that is the most important thing for me in the short term?" It was lots of pairs of knickers, so I filled the microwave, which I could just about carry and put it in the car and left.

Jo Havell b. 1943

Homosexuality may be frowned on in some quarters and marriage is not an option for a couple of the same sex who wish to make a lasting commitment:

My marital status is quite interesting. Technically I'm single because the law doesn't allow 'poofters' to get married does it? But in fact we've been together for nineteen years and two years ago we had our own ceremony. I would consider myself extremely married to Peter. A friend of mine runs a hotel which is really nice and we wanted to have the ceremony there - amazingly she said, "No charge"! What we did was set up a table with things on it, like wine, a white cloth, gifts we were going to exchange. Neither of us is a person who thought it was a terribly good idea to make promises and vows because they tie you down to who you are now, so we wanted to leave ourselves as much freedom as possible. We asked ourselves

59

why we were doing this and decided we wanted to say to everybody around us, friends, relatives, that this relationship is really important to us. We've been together for seventeen years and it feels better than it ever did, so it was very much a "why I am with you" ceremony.

Geoff Hardy b. 1950

If you look back to 1980 when Peter and I met. It was a very 'right on' time. I'm not being derogatory. I do laugh at some of the things I said and did then but, never the less, I think it was a very important time where we challenged a lot of things. We got terribly serious. We didn't want to ape heterosexuality. You didn't do things like that - 'they' got married and 'we' didn't. But after about ten years we started to celebrate anniversaries and that felt really nice, and gradually it just dawned on us that it would be good to share this with everybody else ... It was important to say that we have a family. There was no dissention at all, everybody was really pleased to be there.

Geoff Hardy b. 1950

Incumbent of Linley Hall, Justin Coldwell looks to the future:

As a family, a lot of them married rather late. I'm biding my time, I'm not leaving it too late I hope ... Country life is much happier in a partnership than on your own ... it's very nice having the dogs around but you sort of long for company.

Justin Coldwell b. 1953

When I was a young man the idea was to get a girl into bed and then not marry her because she was easy - or, if you got her pregnant, marry her definitely. Suddenly (with the pill) girls could do that too, and it changed society enormously.

Merrick Roocroft b. 1937

Joyce Brand met and married her first love:

I was offered the opportunity of having a state scholarship to go to Oxford University. But then I met the man I was going to marry and education seemed of little interest, so I abandoned all of that. We were both young socialists - in those days it was called The League of Youth - and he was the treasurer, organising fund-raising dances. I was nearly seventeen and fired with the idea of politics being able to offer a solution to some of the ills of the world. I don't believe that now, and haven't for a very long time, but I believed it passionately in those days.

60

Was he your first lover?

Indeed he was, and I was absolutely, totally and utterly besotted with him. I experienced that feeling of not being able to sleep, thinking about nothing except him and wanting to ditch absolutely everything ... and it is a grand feeling isn't it.

What did you do together in terms of 'going out'?

The first thing we did together (in 1950) was to go to hear a performance of Faust and I was just overwhelmed. I couldn't believe that music like that had been going on and I didn't know anything about it!

What was your first marital home like?

Well, I married him whilst he was doing National Service and he was posted out to North Africa and I couldn't conceive of the idea of not seeing him for any period of time so I cashed all of our savings - he had £470 and I had £5! - and followed him out to Libya. Our first married home was a small flat in Benghazi.

Joyce Brand b. 1934

Don Stokes trod a dangerous path in his courting days:

In 1946 there was quite a keen tennis club in Ellesmere and one of the girl tennis players was Mary, a member of the Young Farmers Club who sponsored the club. Her father was a dairy farmer too. At the time I was courting another girl two nights a week but when I met Mary I rang her up one day and asked if she had a boyfriend. She said "No", so I took her out as well, so I could compare a blonde with a brunette.

That was a bit of a dangerous thing to do in place like Ellesmere, wasn't it?

It was, yes. Even father told me I mustn't do things like that. He was a rather old fashioned sort and he said, "One at a time. Never two at once. It's rather a dangerous formula!"

Were you found out?

Yes.

How?

Somehow through the grapevine I think. Somebody reported they'd seen the other girl in the car. Obviously there was a bit of heartache when you had to discard one for the other. You could be freer talking with one compared to the other who was rather old fashioned in her thoughts and who wouldn't use make up. So all the time you were sizing them up as to which was the best. And in 1949 I married Mary.

And would Mary have been your first lover?

Nearly!

Don Stokes b. 1923

61

Sometimes there's the odd trick to be played by the ladies:

> My grandfather didn't want my aunts to be late coming home.
> When they went out he would light a candle in the hall, and in
> the morning come down to see how much had burned away
> so he knew what time they'd come in. But they discovered what
> he was doing and put a new candle in!
>
> **Hugo Jones b. 1910**

Gordon Perks reaffirmed his vows on his wedding anniversary:

> After fifty years we wanted to go back to Pontesbury Church and
> take out vows again. July 29 was on a Thursday - the same day as
> our wedding day. The vicar wanted us to go on a Sunday which
> was August 2 - which was my birthday. The family got together
> and decided to put on something for us. The first thing we knew
> about it was when we got to the church just before the service.
> They were all there. We took our vows again after the service
> and Margaret had a new wedding ring because it had worn so
> thin after fifty years.
>
> **Gordon Perks b. 1929**

Margaret Perks tells her side of the story:

> My wedding ring was 34/6 from a place on the Cop and I had
> to get it myself because Gordon wasn't here. When we went
> to get a new one the man laughed and laughed and laughed.
> He said it had worn very well.
>
> **Margaret Perks b. 1928**

CHAPTER 6
CRIME & THE LAW

Has crime increased over the century? It appears to have risen dramatically but could this just be perception and media coverage? From the village bobby and the drunk brass band through to the Shrewsbury red light district, there are stories of scrumping, burglary, murders, mayhem and drug dealing, with tales from both sides of the fence.

> **I'd like to be a policeman or a garden designer. I'm balancing between the two.**
>
> **Darren Fountain b. 1987**

Gordon Perks described a brush with the law in the 1930s:

We moved in 1938 to Kennel Lane [Annscroft]. They had beautiful fruit trees next to the school garden. One night after school - in we went - scrumping. We couldn't get out because they'd put a fence over the wall but there was a big gate and we were scrambling under it when we both got stuck with our pockets full of apples and pears - and who should come but the local bobby. He grabbed hold of the back of our necks and pulled us out saying, "Now take all the apples down to your father, tell him what you've done and tell him to dish out the punishment" - that was a cut across the legs with the birch. "Bring all the apples back to the school in the morning and I'll be there with the boss and if your father hasn't given you enough punishment, I will and the boss will." Before we left he gave us a clip across the ear. That's how punishment was dealt with then.

Gordon Perks b. 1929

> **Two or three of us would go scrumping and I'd hide the apples or pears inside my knickers.**
>
> **Muriel Painter b. 1925**

Dennis Crowther, poet, musician and monologist was a little older when he fell foul of the Boys in Blue:

I was very nearly locked up once. I was a porter on the Ludlow Racecourse. I was sent there from the dole office. I walked there and gave the man my ticket on the gate and he put a white overall on me with 'porter' all across the front. He gave

63

me a tray and said, "Your job is to take fancy cakes and pies from Tattersalls down to the Owners' and Trainers' tent". Well I was travelling down the racecourse with my tray of doughnuts and I met a gang of men off the Clee Hill who were about half cut - and they hadn't had anything to eat so they eat every doughnut I'd got in the middle of Ludlow racecourse. I pondered the question - shall I go back to the man on the gate and report this, or go to the Owner and Trainer's tent and tell them what's happened. I decided to go to the man on the gate who instantly dismissed me. That job lasted ten minutes. He had my gown and tray off me and told me to get lost. He'd had people like me off the dole before. I was walking from there to Ludlow when a police van pulled up. A man had broken into a shop in Craven Arms - a tall man with a limp - looked much like me I expect because they put me in the back and took me to Ludlow. Superintendent Taylor said, "Let that man go - that's Crowther he's entertaining us tomorrow night"

Dennis Crowther b. 1926

He also has a tale to tell about the local policeman:

There was a policemen in Cleobury (Mortimer) and he turned all the brass band out of the pub because we were after time and when we all came out he stopped there all night himself and came out drunk the next morning.

Dennis Crowther b. 1926

Dorothy Lutner talked about the scrumping in Market Drayton:

There were three little boys that lived in Frog Lane. They used to go playing together in the road. Then one day they found some beautiful apples - so they were going in night after night - eating the apples. One night Jack Malkin said, "there's somebody watching us". "Yes I've got you now!" - it was Bobby Turner. He caught one of the boys and he wanted him to tell him the other boys names - but he wouldn't tell. There was a police station just across the road and he said, "We'll take you to the police station and see what the Sergeant says". He got two of the names out of him. One was the policeman's son. He gave him a good scolding and said, "Now look, if you do this again I'm going to lock you up."

Dorothy Lutner b. 1899

*The image of the village bobby and the youngsters scrumping
fade before the horror of crimes of national significance:*

> David Blakeley was at school with me, exactly the same age, and
> I knew him quite well. I must admit I didn't like him very much.
> He was the person who was murdered by his girlfriend. He was
> shot outside a pub in Islington in the fifties by Ruth Ellis, the last
> woman to be hanged for murder.
>
> **Were you shocked?**
>
> It rather shook me that someone I knew had been murdered,
> and then when one knew what had been going on in the
> background - rather horrified the girl was hanged. I've always
> been against capital punishment.
>
> **John Oliver b. 1929**

> After the war Shrewsbury was intensively policed - we had
> four beats inside the river, so there were four policemen
> walking about inside the bridges. There were three others
> cycling around on the outside. Local knowledge was tremendous.
> I recall a lovely phrase from an old policeman, "I closed with
> him Your Worship and he fell to the ground" - no other
> explanation was needed! The old Borough men liked their
> beer. I remember going out with one dear old lad. You'd wet
> your finger and run it up the pane. It would squeak and the
> licensee would come and open the back door and you went
> in and had a couple of pints - if he'd gone to bed, he'd leave
> it by the drain at the back of the pub.
>
> **Richard Blythe b. 1926**

Richard Blythe also had a tale to tell about Cleobury Mortimer:

> As part of my probationary training I moved from Shrewsbury
> to Cleobury Mortimer for three months. It was smashing.
> The Sergeant was an elderly policeman who was one of those
> characters. His language was foul to everybody but he was first
> up in the morning and the last to go to bed. In his seventies
> he was nursing a fractured wrist from punching somebody at
> a dance. A lad let off a firework at the cinema in Cleobury,
> it was during the film 'Scott of the Antarctic' and he was
> taken down to the police station and formally banished from
> Cleobury Mortimer. "You are not to come back to Cleobury
> until I say so." About a month later I got a telephone call from
> this lad saying: "Will you ask the Sergeant if I can come back
> to town please?"
>
> **Richard Blythe b. 1926**

Della Bailey was not sure about her father's 'profession':

I used to think my dad was something to do with spying (this was in 1938). I had to go round to the local policeman ... and say "the moon will be right tonight". I had to go to the verger and a man who'd got a good job at the pit. Those people didn't need to go poaching but they loved to go poaching with my dad.

He [my father] wouldn't teach my two brothers to poach. He said, "I had to do it because I'd got no money and seven hungry kids. But there's plenty of work for you". He was very strict about the law. You didn't touch anything that didn't belong to you.

Della Bailey b 1926

Poaching wasn't that severe after the war. The legislation was Victorian and was an example of the hereditary Peers making sure they had their sport. Before the war country policemen were inclined to be viewed as part of the lord of the manor's staff - the evening's point duty used to be outside the hall or manor.

Richard Blythe b. 1926

Although we may look back through 'rose coloured spectacles' to a more gentle society Beryl Gower points out there were things going on - even in the county town!

Only twenty years ago I was standing waiting for my husband - every week I used to go to the music society which I ran in Shrewsbury. I realised these men were coming round in cars I didn't know what they were doing. A police car stopped and he said, "Are you waiting for someone - I don't think you'd better wait here - you know there are kerb crawlers", and I said, "Pardon?" That was my education in my sixties that this was starting in Shrewsbury. I was out by the market, just round the corner from Shoplatch in Barker Street - by the bus station. A car came round three times, with three men in it. I thought this was a bit odd - then the police came round. I was shaking like a jelly when I realised I 'd made myself so vulnerable.

Beryl Gower b. 1918

And Ray Wagg agreed:

We talk of violence these days, I frequently got knocked about outside the Music Hall in Shrewsbury on a Saturday night, by gang warfare. Youths from the Ditherington area mixing with youths from the Monkmoor area for example, if you went in to try to quell it either side would delight in giving you a good beating - this would be in the early sixties.

Ray Wagg b. 1941

Colin Painter was angry about the injustice of prosecuting people for helping themselves to the odd log or two:

I remember in about 1943 a tree blew down in Berwick Road, blocking it. The neighbours there went down with saws and helped themselves to wood from the tree. Either the council or the landowner, I forget which, prosecuted them for taking the wood away. I thought that was disgusting. The people were taken to court and fined. I thought that was a terrible injustice considering the tree was blocking the road anyway. The police went round the houses to see if they could find the wood. They would only have taken away what they could carry.

Colin Brown b 1931

But not all crimes are perceived in exactly the same light:

I remember some odd spinster ladies who lived way out on the road to Welshpool. I had to cycle all the way out there and their complaint was that their next door neighbours had killed a pig and left a barrowfull of entrails on the footpath. They were constantly falling out with their neighbours - I said, "What can you see? I can't see anything" and they said, "Well if you stand on a chair and look out of the window you can see over the hedge." It was a pair of houses and they'd had trouble before. The Judge in the Civil Court had insisted on a white line being painted down the tiles and the wall so they knew which was their house and which was their neighbour's house. They were a real nuisance.

Richard Blythe b. 1926

Richard Blythe talked about the credibility of the police force and how it had become reduced by the problems of the miners' strike in the 1980s:

The police force was used in a non-legal way. To prevent miners moving from one area to another. They were stopped on main roads from getting to places. The clashes that developed seemed to me to be against all the principles of the police force. We did a lot of riot training and that was unusual ... as if we were being prepared. But we had had the winter of discontent. I thought "a plague on both their houses" in a way.

Richard Blythe b. 1926

Ray Wagg presents a different view:

They're fantastic people the mining community, but I didn't resent being used in the political sense because I felt, and still do, such major disruption of other people lives was not justified by Arthur Scargill and the way they behaved. When you consider police columns were having paving slabs thrown off road bridges on top of them on our way to police a particular pit and the abuse that would come from otherwise decent sort of chaps, I didn't like that, but I didn't think it all a politician's fault. I simply said there is no reason why this man or this woman should behave in this way towards us.

Ray Wagg b. 1941

> **When we finally passed out at Police College we had to do traffic duty to the Blue Danube. So many of waving traffic from the left, waving traffic from the right in sync with the music which was played over a loudspeaker.**
>
> **Ray Wagg b. 1941**

When I was first a magistrate, when the witness or the accused came before the court, he'd been given an oath to read. And nearly everybody was able to read it. As the years have passed by, many, many young men - aged 18-20 - have been unable to read the oath. The clerk of the court has to read it for them and they repeat it. This, to me, is a really startling development that so many youngsters who get into trouble can't actually read. When in the old days everybody seemed to be able to read, if falteringly.

Don Stokes b. 1923

Does the Devil make work for idle hands?

When we lived in Broseley, right in the middle of the town, the square was filled all day long and most of the night with young people smoking and drinking. Drugs were going on up there, too, but basically just sitting around. They had nothing to do and nowhere to go. The buses weren't running, they'd been cut down. There was nothing for them.

Bill Caddick b. 1944

Looking back on the police force Richard Blythe drew some conclusions:

> By today's standards the police force probably wasn't very efficient but by the standards of the time, the local knowledge and what was going on - and there wasn't much going on - I remember a house being broken into in Shelton one night and when we on duty the next day it was spoken of in a whisper as if it was a serious incident. We weren't even told where it was. There was an atmosphere that crime was very serious and had to be dealt with very seriously.
>
> **Richard Blythe b. 1926**

Drugs have become today's bete noir. From the 'soft drugs' of the sixties we have moved into the land of designer drugs - designed to appeal to a young market:

> With drugs at first it was curiosity, but then it's not, because it just grabs you. Everyone says you don't want to smoke - that it'll take a grip of you and you think, "No, I can handle it" but you can't. All of a sudden it's got you and there's nothing you can do about it. You go out and steal for it, do anything. And that's when I started doing commercial burglaries, stealing computers, which I've been doing for the past seven years. I'd come off drugs, I was just drinking and drinking but you just spend as much money, wasting money. I'm just standing round, just drinking. I'd spend a couple of hundred pounds drinking, buying drinks, buying a draw ... If you're used to having money all the time the stealing becomes something you need. If you haven't got it, it's like you've lost something.
>
> **Eamon Daly b. 1975**

> These days I'd just keep away from everything. People say, "Oh ecstasy - great - I'll go out and boogie all night" - I'd be frightened to death.
>
> **Squirrel b. 1951**

When I became the Telford's police drugs officer in 1978 it was a busy job. There were about eight serious drug dealers in the area and I dealt with them all at one time or another. I saw my first real drug addicts in the seventies. I dealt with people I felt more sorry for than anything else.

How did the police go about responding to that early drugs problem?

Arrest as many as we could and lock them up. But that didn't solve the problem and we should have known that at the time really.

Terry Lowe b. 1943

Serving time in Shrewsbury Prison for Burglary, Eamon Daly described some of the things he had done:

We started doing robberies after the joyriding. Shops, cash and carries. Some of the things I've done you wouldn't believe. I went to the outdoor - the off licence - one night. We knew there was money in the safe in the back, me and my mate. There was a counter and a cage that went up from the counter to within a foot of the ceiling. We climbed over and there was a woman in there, screaming. I'll never forget it. I went into the back to get the money out of the safe and when I came out she was fighting with my friend. My friend turned round and hit her and we came out of the shop. The woman was in a coma for two weeks. After that I never did another shop robbery. I felt guilty even though it wasn't me who actually hit her - I was there. I spent the money on crack, cannabis and drink.

Eamon Daly b. 1975

Being a victim of crime is upsetting in the extreme. Della Bailey described her feelings:

When I was burgled the first time, it hurt. I was hurt because I thought, "why me?" I thought, "I wouldn't take anything belonging to anybody, why have they done that to me?" The third time I was burgled I sold the place. I was in despair because ... they'd taken useless things. I think I wept more about those than anything else. The pink pin out of my daughter's nappy and the blue pin out of my son's. What on earth good were they to them? But to me they meant a lot.

Della Bailey b. 1926

Former policeman Richard Blythe had also experienced the feeling:

I had my car stolen. It was found and I disconnected the battery because it had been damaged. I called the garage to pick it up, but when they got there it had been stolen again. I was a bit annoyed about that.

Richard Blythe b. 1926

My first day's duty at Shrewsbury Police station on Swan Hill was to dust all the lampshades and then make the sergeant's cup of tea at seven o'clock. I was on earlies in those days - six o'clock start, but we had to be on duty a quarter of an hour before that for parade purposes. Parade was in effect a sort of military manoeuvre - you had to produce your handcuffs, your truncheon, to prove you'd got them - although I never used my truncheon ever.

Ray Wagg b. 1941

Richard Blythe remembered back to the time when the majority of arrests were for "drunk and disorderly" or "drunk and incapable".

I arrested a young man - he'd driven into the back of a Midland Red Bus and he had his Great Dane in the car with him. I took him into the police station followed by this Great Dane which promptly leapt up and put its paws on the shoulders of the Sergeant - who was frightened to death. We put the young man in the cells for being drunk, and the Great Dane in a police car and took it home - all the way to Bicton or somewhere.

Richard Blythe b. 1926

The day war broke out we were all standing on the bridge at the bottom of Kennel Lane boasting about what we were going to do with the Germans. Again I felt a tug on my collar - it was the policeman. He clipped me round the ear and pulled a catapult out of my back pocket. He said, "And how many Germans do you think you're going to kill with this?" I never saw the catapult again.

Gordon Perks b. 1929

In all my years in the police force I only ever pulled my truncheon out once.

Terry Lowe b. 1943

Now, I'll guarantee there isn't a constable walking round Shrewsbury on the beat tonight, walking round town, looking at what's going on, smelling what's going on, listening to what's going on. There'll be some TV cameras, the man might be watching the monitor but there's no contact. When we were walking round the streets young men saw us and knew that if their conduct persisted they would be spoken to. There was no running around the streets shouting and yahooing because somebody would see them and deal with them. So there was quite a tight control of the street and movement on the street. It's gone. So young bloods can behave in any way they wish and it gets to the point where it's beyond control and they have to get in 2, 3, 4, 5, 6 Police officers to deal with it.

Richard Blythe b. 1926

And is prison the deterrent we once believed it to be?

It' so weird having a TV in your cell now. It's not jail anymore, is it? How can you rehabilitate anybody when they've got a TV in their cell? When I first started jail, years ago, it was Borstals or Detention Centres and once you'd done a sentence in one of those you went out and you thought, "I don't want to do that again." But now you come in here and you stroll through it. You only get banged up for two or three hours a day ... and you've got a tele to be banged up with. If it wasn't for missing my children, and the new life I now want to lead, this wouldn't deter me doing whatever I wanted to do when I got out. In my old job, all this feels like to me now is working away from home. And that's all it is. There's nothing hard. In borstals, years ago, they used to make you do circuits and make you scrub landings all day long. They'd give you a scrubbing brush and they used to call this corridor "the motorway" and it seemed to take for ever to scrub it. Now that deterred you. But this is getting too soft now.

Paul Taylor b. 1967

When drugs first came about the police came in and gave we Magistrates a lecture on the different types. We all had a little sniff of everything as it was passed round to see what it was all about and we thought, "Oh , it'll never come to Shrewsbury".

Ray Parker J.P. b. 1929

In the end you've got to respect what the police do, keeping people like us off the streets.

Paul Taylor b. 1967

The next few quotes come from Alan Bramley, Prison Governor at Shrewsbury Prison:

You mustn't dismiss the importance of a ten year heroin habit when you're only twenty years of age. That means you started to use smack when you were ten, at school. And we've got hundreds of examples in this town of kids in that position.

And if we don't even attempt to provide therapy and counselling support programmes for people who have got substance dependency problems, then we're just storing up trouble for the day they're released. They'll just go back to robbing you and me to feed a habit that we could have done something about - and chose not to.

He continued:

From the sixties on, amongst youngsters, there's been this increasing need to find a way to get a buzz. We felt we were breaking the rules when we had a pint of beer when we were seventeen and a half ... and that was really quite adventurous behaviour. But then rules ceased to be terribly significant and people began to seek ways of breaching bigger rules. The pop music industry suddenly saw among its icons all the enormously wealthy nineteen year olds absolutely stoned out of their minds in public the whole time and, frankly, it was socially acceptable. Like drink driving. In those days if somebody was caught by a policeman driving over the limit it was, "how unfortunate to be caught". And it was with the same kind of libertarian approach that a pop star being locked up in San Francisco overnight for being in possession of some opium-based substance was just a good giggle. That fed down through television and magazines into the minds of the kids who regarded pop stars as heroes. A seed was sown which said it wasn't that bad actually to break the rules.

Then the criminals stepped in?
Well, they would wouldn't they, if there's a few bob to be made easily out of a new trend. The profit margins in drugs have always been astonishing, and they still are today. Criminals are essentially feckless, greedy opportunists.

Alan Bramley b. 1948.

Times have moved on so fast and there have been so many changes:

Responsibility for drinking and driving was only just coming in. At Cleobury they did catch a farmer, of course there were no breathalysers in those days, you had to get a doctor to come and certify. But before the court appearance the farmer shot himself. It was that much of a stigma.

Richard Blythe b. 1926

The last word:

I would not advise my grandson to go into the police force. I wouldn't want to go in now, or if I did I'd choose carefully where I went, like the north of Scotland or somewhere - Penzance probably. I think life's too vicious now. Violence occurs so quickly and knives and firearms are becoming more used. I don't ever recall seeing a firearm and people just didn't carry knives.

Richard Blythe b. 1926

CHAPTER 7
GROWING UP

*Childhood today is almost unrecognisable from the way it was
at the beginning of the century - the childhood which our
parents, grandparents and great grandparents experienced.
There were no computers, video games, television - and
childhood seemed to be much shorter. Many people at the
beginning of the century left school aged 13 or 14 and began
work. It was also very unusual for women to continue into
higher education. Change came gradually, the Second World
War becoming a watershed and the 1960s bringing the advent
of a new generation - the teenager. Today, growing up happens
at a much faster rate. Family life has changed beyond recognition
and education is an opportunity to gain qualifications for a
career. Here are some of the experiences of Shropshire people
beginning with some childhood memories:*

> **Childhood is something that happened after the war.**
> **Brian Barrett b. 1929**

I remember the dark winter morning in Shrewsbury and the
man shouting "hot rolls" as he carried them around. On a Good
Friday his message would change from "hot rolls" to "hot cross
buns". The sounds I can remember, and the appearance of the
old gaslighter with his long pole coming to light the lamp outside
where we lived, and coming first thing in the morning to switch
it off again.

Gordon Riley b. 1922

I grew up very happily on Woodside (Telford). Going back I see
it very differently, but as a child I perhaps just didn't see there
were people who were quite underprivileged.

Katherine Soutar b. 1963

I remember my father in uniform looking strange and kissing me
and telling me to look after my mother, before going off to the
first World War.

Emma Bullock b. 1911

Dorothy Lutner remembered her first school day in Market Drayton:

My mum took me to school and I thought, "what a great big
building". There was a big iron gate with spikes on the top that
surrounded the school. We knocked on the door and the

Headmistress came. I had to take off my coat, hat and gloves in the cloakroom where there was a very large slate sink and a tap with cold water. From there we walked into the classroom.

Dorothy Lutner b. 1899

Poverty meant books were a luxury for some children:

I was the only reader in my family. My mother's concern was providing us with the next meal. When you're that poor you don't have many books. I used to get what books I had and go into the bathroom - it was the only room with a lock on the door. I'd get a blanket from the airing cupboard and I'd put it in the bath and lie on it and read. I'd read until somebody banged on the door. I think I was fortunate enough to be a clever child. My mother bought me books when she could. You were only allowed one book at a time from the library.

Kathleen Hann b. 1930

and school wasn't necessarily a happy experience for everyone:

> **I was quite badly bullied at school and I became quite peculiar as a defence.**
>
> **Katherine Soutar b. 1963**

I had heaps of boyfriends - I can always remember feeling I preferred the boys to the girls. There was no bullying - we were in one playground - we weren't segregated. The friendship of the boys was probably more important than that of the girls - and basically my only loathing was the severity of the discipline in the school. It was so harsh. I never told my parents. We were hit across the knuckles with a ruler really hard if we didn't get our sums right. This distressed me, it didn't help me, so I came to dread going to school. When I was ten, I walked through the girls' toilet - all the toilets were in the playground - and I caught the geography master and the gym mistress closely embraced in the girls cloakroom. I was so shocked. I rushed out for fear they'd seen me - and they had - I knew they had. I knew the master would take it out on me and he did. The very next lesson was geography. I had to sit next to a naughty boy and help him, and the master picked up the biggest book he could find on his desk - walked slowly towards me - I knew he was coming to me and he asked me a question I couldn't answer - I got it wrong and he swiped the back of my head as hard as he could so I fell upon the desk - and I refused to produce a tear. He did that four times and the boy on my right was muttering, "I'll get him!" I held my head up - the door opens and who walks in but my own sister who happened to see the last hit I got. She hands the master a note and never even glanced at me. At the end of the lesson I was asked to go and see the headmaster so my sister had witnessed it and went straight to the headmaster and reported it. I still remember his words - he got hold of my hand and said "has this ever happened before? Your sister's told me everything. The master has been dismissed". I was half wanting to cry with the emotion. He said, "We're sending for your mother and you can go home - you can come into the restroom now". That was my first experience of corporal punishment from a master with a girl and that shattered me. It made me feel I'm going to be a fighter - it left a deep seated feeling in my heart that I will probably never forget.

Beryl Gower b. 1918

Geoff Hardy was singled out as being different and bullied:

It wasn't until I was about thirteen or fourteen that I started to get the "Backs against the wall, Hardy's coming!" at school. I can remember most weeks, throwing-up on the way to school. It was fear, fear that this was going to happen, that I was going to be singled out again for being gay.

Geoff Hardy b. 1950

I loved school. Pontesbury school was a great place. I know it was better if you went to the grammar school and we passed the exam to go to the Priory but you know, the thing was, there wasn't enough money. My mum and dad couldn't afford to send me there. If we'd have passed the scholarship where they paid for everything it would have been different but that year there wasn't many scholarships. There was no way that they could afford the uniform, books and travel so I didn't go. But I felt I had a really good education at Pontesbury - it was a good school.

Evelyn Hatton b. 1926

I remember sitting in my desk. The teachers were very strict (they were Welsh). A teacher was marking my book and I was eating my jam sandwiches. She found I'd made a mistake so she got off her chair in the dinnertime and came down to me and pushed a pencil in my ribs till the jam squirted out all over my face.

Dennis Crowther b. 1926

I didn't have a lot of toys. I never knew what a doll was when I was little.

Nellie Rowson b. 1914

I used to go to the village school until I was eleven, at Weston Rhyn. I had to stop at the station and wait for the fast train to come through just after four o'clock from Liverpool to Shrewsbury. They threw a bundle of Liverpool Echoes out and I had to get an Echo to take home for my father to keep up with what was happening in the First World War because there was no radio or telephone or that sort of thing.

Edgar Gibbs b. 1908

One of my first memories of the British School in Ludlow was playing in the playground - it must have been in 1940 - and seeing the soldiers coming to a rest home in Ludlow from Dunkirk. Then a year or two later we were thrilled when the American convoys used to go up Old Street and throw sweets and chewing gum. Situated as my family was, right in the heart of the town, we were aware of the very lively nightlife Ludlow had during the war, much of it emanating from the camps down at Ludford. First the RAF had a training camp there and then the Americans, who were very popular with local people -particularly the girls - but they sometimes had the most dreadful fights in town. My father was a police constable and was called out to deal with them. I remember on one occasion a weighing machine was thrown through our shop window, which terrified us.

David Lloyd b. 1935

Just as the population of London was being evacuated to the country at the start of the Second World War, Brian Barrett was sent from the country to London to the Freemason's school:

The Freemason's School was a very good boarding school to be fair, but it was a pre-war type boarding school with quite a harsh regime. Of course it was wartime which might have made it slightly better in terms of diet. Before the war the school diet was carved on tablets of stone at the beginning of the term, but with the war of course you couldn't do that. If there were eggs available you got an egg, irrespective of what the diet sheet said. It was a fairly harsh sort of life. I wouldn't put any of my children through it - not going to boarding school at the age of eight ... going to boarding school was a fairly traumatic experience. With hindsight I realise how traumatic it was. You go from a village and a little school of forty or fifty all age pupils in it and you finish up at a school of 800 on the outskirts of London, with the war starting so that it got bombed occasionally.

Brian Barrett b. 1929

Jo Havell's early years were spent in Australia and she found it difficult to fit in when she returned to England:

It was very difficult settling back into Britain. Very cold, wearing school uniform, realising that words I said which were colloquialisms in Australia were swear words here, and the place I chose to do it for the first time was when the Headmistress of my school asked me, "What do you think of the weather dear?" My response was, "It's a fair cow, isn't it Miss?" The look of horror on her face will always make me smile.

Jo Havell b. 1943 ———

When I was getting near to the top of the school and one of the teachers was away, they used to ask one of the girls to sit in with the class. They were given work to do, and if they were making heavy weather of it I used to give them a little help and I enjoyed it. I felt that I was successful. I don't know whether I was, but that made me feel teaching was what I wanted to do. I didn't know if I'd ever get that far.

Mary Hignett b. 1912

Squirrel wanted to rebel:

I wanted to grow my hair - I hated short, back and sides. It was a constant battle. Mostly with my step-father. My mum married him when I was about six. I hated him from the word go - and I still do. He was a bully. He was the one who wanted me to look like a 'dork'. He was a lovely person to rebel against. He took me on as a step-child. Then they had a family. I've got half brothers and a sister. I don't really contact them. I'd probably cause trouble with them.

Squirrel b. 1951

My parents don't have to discipline me as long as I keep to my dad's rules.

Darren Fountain b. 1987

Perhaps a return to National Service isn't really the answer:

National Service taught me to be lazy. Anybody who's talking about National Service and tells the truth will tell you that they'd walk round for hours carrying clip boards and looking smart, but never actually did anything except hang around and wait for the next meal. You also got so fit that you were released upon the unsuspecting population full of beans, and after four or five pints all hell used to let loose from the pubs on a Saturday night. But I came out still a virgin.

Merrick Roocroft b. 1937

We had little in the way of toys and children would run miles when there was a pig killing to get the pig's bladder which the butcher would blow up with a straw so it could be used as a football. A much prized article. One little boy approached my father who was assisting at a pig killing and said, "Is this a girl pig or a boy pig?" Dad looked at him and said, "Well actually it's a girl pig", and the little boy said, "I am disappointed! Girl pigs don't have bladders do they?"

Emily Griffiths b. 1917

Alan J Gardner remembered a very exciting experience from his childhood:

My father, being in the telephone service, was very interested in radio, and I think we must have had the first crystal sets in our area, even before the BBC started up properly. Anyway, Children's Hour ran a story competition and I was one of four prize winners. So I was able to get permission from school to have the afternoon off so I could go home and be scrubbed and put on my best suit, an Eton collar and a clip-on bow tie. I was told not to ride on top of the bus and to get off at Charring Cross and ask a policemen for directions to Savoy Hill where the studio was. But I did ride on top of the bus so my hair was dishevelled by time I got there. All the buses were open-topped then. I showed the policemen my letter. He was very impressed that I was going to the BBC so he stepped out into the road, held up his hand and stopped all of London's traffic for me. He crossed the road with me and directed me on to Savoy Hill. The Commisionaire at the entrance directed me up the stairs to the first floor. Here I met Uncle Caractacus, Aunt Sophie, and Uncle Lesley who were all dressed in evening dress with winged collars and real bow ties (not clip-on ones like mine). I was led into the studio where there were four chairs for the four prize winners. Apart from that, the only furniture was a grand piano pushed to one end and the microphone which was housed in an enormous great box on wheels and they had to stand to speak directly into it. Then just before five, Uncle Arthur walked in. He was Arthur Burrows, the chief announcer of the BBC at the time and he pushed scripts into the hands of the others. He warned us four children to be silent and the broadcast started with the words "Hello Children". Now towards the end of every Children's Hour each day there would be greetings read out to children who had their birthday on that day. They'd take turns to read them - first one Uncle, then an Aunt and so on. But when it came to twins, all their heads would poke forward and they'd say "Hello twins" all together. Of course, seeing their heads poked forward out of these winged collars all together made me snigger and titter. Uncle Arthur held up his finger to remonstrate with me. That was the first time I was 'On the Air' - not just to Shropshire but to the whole of England.

Alan J Gardner b. 1912

Nesta Cheadle's garden was an imaginary school room:

My sister Nesta was always playing schools in the garden with rows of cabbages and Brussels sprouts as the pupils. She would sit on a chair and teach the cabbages. She'd belt hell out of these cabbages with a cane. My father would come home and find all the leaves on the ground. So we used to have to pick them all up before he got home. In mother's shop we had an enamel cupboard in which we kept the butter and the bacon in a cool place. The enamel top was white so Nesta marked black lines on it with charcoal or chalk and that would be her pretend piano. She'd play away, singing along on this imaginary piano.

Alf Cheadle b. 1922

When the Snailbeach Mines closed my father took over the stewardship of the local Home Office explosives magazine, which was the old powder magazine which had been used for the Tankerville Mine. He used to take explosives to the Hagleth Mines over the hills from here with a pony and trap because you were not allowed to transport high explosives except in a specially constructed vehicle - not a mechanically propelled vehicle with sparks and petrol involved. Also farmers could get a police licence to collect, say, ten pounds of explosives to blow up tree roots. So there always had to be someone at home anytime during the hours of daylight to go up to the magazine, about a mile and a half away, and collect these explosives for the farmers. I would have to go because my father was working and my mother was ill. I've gone on my bicycle many a time and carried ten pounds worth of gelignite down the front of my coat.

Emily Griffiths b. 1917

Parents could be so embarrassing:

My dad had lots of fluffy hair and a beard and my mum had long hair and wore long skirts. She wore her hair in bunches for a long time and I remember my sister saying, "Could you not come to school with your hair in bunches."

Katherine Soutar b. 1963

We used to have to wait for a birthday to come round to have a particular book as a treat. I know that sounds old fashioned and carping - I don't mean it to - I'm not in the slightest bit resentful of the goodies children have now, but I do see them bewildered by the richness of experience which is thrown at them and although they mature apparently much more quickly than we did - they certainly loose their innocence in all sorts of ways very quickly. I don't see them happy. I see an awful lot of children overweight, unfit and dissatisfied - and yet they are in homes which give them everything.

Elaine Bruce b. 1938

Adolescence was the world of music in the 60s

I was into more underground music than The Beatles and there were more messages coming through. There was a movement called Foreshore - I wanted to be part of it. I was always being pushed to get that vital piece of paper that landed you a good job, or you'd end up digging the road for the council, or in the army. The army was the dregs then. Anybody who joined the army, they didn't know anything. They joined the army because there was nothing left. I thought piece of paper - job - you've got to have something to fall back on. Then I thought - I'm not going to fall back. Jimi Hendrix said, "straight ahead", and at the time there was so much going on in the music - the messages in the music and music meant more to me than anything the teachers could tell me - or my family. I couldn't switch my brain off. I knew there was much, much more in the world.

Squirrel b. 1951

I worked at the cinemas in Cosford, then I moved on to the Air Ministry there, as an electricians mate, and from there I volunteered for the RAF when I was seventeen. The recruiting booth was in Beatties in Wolverhampton. I sat down in front of the WAAF Officer to give my details, I wanted to be air crew and do all these wonderful things. A little old lady came up to the recruiting desk and harangued the officer, waving her umbrella at her and telling her how wicked it was that she was taking these young boys to be killed in the war. I thought it was silly - but I can see her point now.

Richard Blythe b. 1926

I never had a hand laid on me by my mother or father - neither did my brother - but I think he could have done with it!

Beryl Gower b. 1918

Dad taught me not to judge. Some children and young people must think it's a crime to be young, but it's not a crime and if you can't have your giddy, carefree days when you're young when can you have them. As long as you don't do terrible things.

Della Bailey b. 1928 ———

New technology helps Miranda Richer keep in touch with her father:

My parents have split up and my dad now lives in Germany. Tomorrow I'm going to Germany for the first time to see him. I quite scared because I don't know anything about Germany except for the war and the Berlin Wall. We used to just speak on the phone once a week, but now we've got the Internet I can E-mail him when I like and he can E-mail me. I know more about what he's up to now by E-mail. It's weird. It's a bit strange getting an E-mail from your dad rather than seeing him, but I've got used to it. We chat about anything I've got up to - what I've done at college, what I get up to at the weekend. It's a lot quicker than writing a letter.

Miranda Richer b. 1982

My father fell ill with duodenal ulcers for 9 to 10 months in 1948, so I had to run the grocer's business (I was in the sixth form at the time) so I decided I might as well stay.

Alex Williams b. 1933

Mary Hignett was about to realise more than her ambitions:

I thought I'd end up just as a pupil teacher. When the time came for the scholarships I didn't know what to say to the headmistress when she asked if I wanted to go in for it. So she said, "Would you like me to speak to your father", and I said, "Oh, yes please." At dinnertime I didn't even like to ask him what he'd decided because I was so afraid he'd be hurt if he had to refuse me. It wasn't that I'd be hurt - it was that he'd be hurt. Then in the afternoon the headmistress came round with the forms and she gave them all out and there wasn't one for me. I just turned away a bit disappointed. I heard my name and she gave me a different coloured one because I was to have one for a university scholarship. I had never dreamt of that. It was one of the thrills of my life, that was.

Mary Hignett b. 1912

> On two occasions I was sent (they had a prisoner of war camp between Gobowen and where we were living, opposite where Moreton Hall School is now) ... I had to collect a soldier with his rifle and two prisoners of war - German prisoners of war - and they used to come and work on the farm. That was towards 1916 -17.
>
> **Edgar Gibbs b. 1908**

Dave Smart believes there should always be healthy competition:

My wife's a school teacher. She teaches physical education and they have to come up with games that are non-competitive. How can you have games that are non-competitive? How can you stop people being competitive. As soon as they leave school they're going into a competitive environment and if they don't compete, they go on Social Security.

Dave Smart b. 1958

We used to get into the pictures when the film was about half over - we'd see it to the end and then we'd see it again all the way through again - we'd stay there until it got to where it was when we came in. Then we'd come out, get "The Picture Goer" paper and come home on the 8 o'clock train to Pontesbury.

Evelyn Hatton b. 1926

> I grew up in a normal suburb estate. It's not like the way it is today. We had more to do when we were kids. We used to play on the waste ground and collect butterflies and all that. But now the kids prefer to go and smash windows. We never used to do that when we were kids.
>
> **Eamon Daly b. 1975**

Mary Stone had an enlightened upbringing:

I never had any barriers in my way at all. I was brought up by a father who believed that everyone should earn their own living regardless of sex or handicap. I married a husband who thought it was grossly unfair that anyone should expect any man to support a woman as well as his children and that women should be earning their own money and living their own life

Mary Stone b.1932

84

But inmate at Shrewsbury prison Eamon Daly had a very different start to life:

> My home wasn't happy, my father used to beat us up - or beat me up I should say. I didn't really stay in much at home once I'd got to the age of twelve or thirteen. I always lived with my aunt or my nan, my uncles and then finally I came into prison when I was fifteen. I've been in and out ever since. I don' know why my father beat me - I haven't a clue to this day. My brother was the favourite of the two of us. My mum did step in at one point, she took me to the doctor and the social services did a report and that was as far as it went. I feel bitter that she didn't take it further, sometimes. I get on fine with my parents now, with my dad, but when I was younger we just didn't hit it off at all.
>
> **Eamon Daly b. 1963**

It was straight from school to work:

> When I left school I was fourteen. I went into service at a farm. You had to do anything there, it was a mixed farm. There wasn't milking but it was mixed like. Rearing calves and cattle and that. I was there for a year and then I went to a farm by Brockton for six months and came down into this village [Aston Munslow]. I've been here ever since.
>
> **Fred Jordan b. 1922**

It seems children do grow up more quickly these days. Kate Lear explains:

> You lose your sense of childhood innocence about nine or ten when you start to know what happens in the world. You start to watch the news and discover everything is not perfect and ideal in the world like you thought it was. Everything was very much centred around you when you were little and you didn't think much about the rest of the world. You just lived in the moment rather than in the future or the past.
>
> **But can you remember watching the news and being made to think about what you saw?**
>
> I remember seeing starving children on the news but I can't remember where they were. I remember being quite shocked, "God! Those people don't have any food". I never thought when I was little that people starved. Why does that happen? In England you can have anything you like to eat. There's ample food and water. How can that happen in our world when we've got so much here?
>
> **Kate Lear b. 1984**

I was almost four years old at the turn of the last century. There was a great sense of jubilation. I had a great admiration of the Queen Victoria. She was grand. I mean, in those days we were Great Britain and that was due to Victoria's ruthless way of sending her soldiers all over the world. I had a grey velvet dress when she died and that was very smart. Mother was in black, certainly, and all the men wore black bands on their arms.

Maisie Thompson b. 1896

CHAPTER 8
GETTING OLDER

How do Shropshire people approach the topic of getting
older? A difficult question because 'old' is how we might
view other people but not a word that we link with ourselves.
When do we get older? Are we happy when we get rid of
the all the teenage angst and sail into our twenties and
thirties. When is it policemen and council officials begin
to look too young to be at work? Is there really such a thing
as 'ageism'? What are the things that change about our
lives as we begin to grow up? The voices of the people of
Shropshire share their secrets.

> **I can have dozens of male friends completely freely -**
> **once you're past sixty they just see you as a person**
> **not a sexual being.**
>
> **Mary Stone b. 1932**

When I was 49 - I'd worked my way up the ladder of journalism
in my terms. Qualified for the job, and there was one step to go.
I was told at the age of 49 I was too old to be editor but would
I stop and teach my successor of 31 how to do it. That's going
back to 1972 and having worked hard to reach the top, I suddenly
fell at the last hurdle. That was the first time I'd experienced ageism.

Gordon Riley b. 1922

> **I was born in the 19th Century and they want me to**
> **try to go through the 20th Century and die in the 21st**
> **Century! I don't know whether I'll do it. I'll be quite a**
> **sensation if I can do it won't I?**
>
> **Dorothy Lutner b. 1899**

Mary Stone believes growing older has freed her:

We live a lot more. I'd never been abroad before I retired.
I'd never flown before - I never thought I would. I was too busy
when I was younger ... the loss of a sense of immortality
probably gives you freedom.

Mary Stone b. 1932

When you were young, at what age did you feel someone
was old?

Oh, about fifty-ish, I should think.

You're ninety. Are you old?

I don't feel any different now than when I finished work, which was in 1974.

Edgar Gibbs b. 1908

I've only begun to feel I was an old person in the last two or three years when my sister started to need waiting on and, quite willingly, I started waiting on her. I found it was too much, so I had to get helpers to come in and then I thought, well, I really am getting old when I can't cope with my own house. But before that I was just going on serenely in the good old way.

Mary Hignett b. 1912

Practicalities prevent you finding freedom - until they no longer worry you:

I wasn't a hippie but I knew a lot of them. Life was very nice seen through their eyes but there was always this feeling that somebody had to get up and sweep the streets. What they realised was what I realised at retirement. That you can begin to live then.

Mary Stone b. 1932

Evelyn Hatton thinks it's a state of mind:

I don't feel old yet. Especially with us going dancing ... My mum only lived until she was 69. I felt a lot younger when I was 69 than mum was. It's amazing when you go to a cemetery and see the gravestones of people who were so old and you realise that they were younger than you are now. It's a bit of a shock. But there won't be any old grandmothers again. I can't imagine my mother at my age now doing keep fit, going dancing and putting on 'lippy' (as I call it) as I do now. There's young people that are old.

Evelyn Hatton b. 1926

I'm going to resign from the youth club this year, at 79 years of age. I think you're aware of your mortality - that you aren't going to go on that much longer. We used to walk a lot in high mountains but we've gradually had to accept that we can no longer do that. I look at Cader Idris every time we go there and I say, "How about having a go?" and my husband says, "For God's sake be realistic, we can't do it". Of course, we probably could do it in the end but it would take a long time.

Cath Marshall b. 1920

> **You are old when you can no longer do what you want to do. When I was a little girl I suppose I thought that people with grey hair were old.**
>
> **Margaret Jones b. 1926**

Modern technology has pretty well passed me by.
Before I retired it hadn't come in and the things I did at home -
getting out into the country and doing some writing for the
Advertiser [Oswestry Advertiser] - they didn't seem to need
this technology. I sent in my scripts for the Advertiser typewritten.
I learned to drive before the war but I'm thinking that maybe
I should finish now, I'm getting a bit old for it. Everybody tells
me I should. Certainly the pace isn't my pace now. I go too
slowly for the youngsters.

Mary Hignett b. 1912

*Sadly, getting older can mean growing away from friends
and partners:*

I think that what we fail to recognise is that in all relationships
as we get older we change and we continue to change, in all
relationships, not just marriage. You grow away from each other,
you have different wants and needs in life and you fail to meet
each other's wants and needs. Sometimes it's so difficult it is
better for everyone involved that you complete the relationship.
It's finished.

Jo Havell b. 1943 ———

Ruth Walmsley is providing a practical solution:

A colleague and I are running workshops in Shropshire on
the menopause. I feel that it is a time when women are feeling
that they can actually do something to help themselves -
they don't have to go into a decline. Middle age means
something very different now. It was sort of perms and bri-
nylon and this was the end of it. Now women of 45 up to 55,
60 are not going downhill but feel they've a new lease of life.
I don't think women look the same as they did. Now you can't
tell how old a woman is from what she is doing or what she
is wearing. People are looking younger and living longer.

Ruth Walmsley b. 1943

John and Jackie Gunton are going to continue to work on their small holding:

> We don't feel superior at all. Partly because we're older, in our fifties now. Frankly we're surviving like anybody else. Keeping going doing what we've done for years. We're not really trying to prove anything anymore. We've found a life that we enjoy and we're going to keep it going as long as we can.
>
> **John and Jackie Gunton b. 1945**

The 'when' of getting older has changed so much over the century:

> My old age differs from that of my parents generation in that they got old, younger. Secondly, they didn't have such a long old age, and thirdly because it was quite difficult to do things. I think they were quite content to sit and be waited on, and there was always the rest of the family living with them who were prepared to wait on them. An eighty year old woman before the war would have thought herself very old. She would probably have been helped to get up in the morning, and then sat in a chair by the fire and had all her wants provided, all her meals provided and be helped back to bed at night. My life is more interesting than most. I get out and see things. I've got to make the effort but, having made the effort, I think it's worth it. There's not a great deal of television that interests me. I have the news on and sometimes that's it.
>
> **Mary Hignett b. 1912**

> I thought people were old when they were fifty. Older women always wore black and had shawls, many didn't have many teeth ... but it depends upon your health and outlook on life. Women go back to work so older women take on the things they used to do.
>
> **Vera Smith b. 1916**

> We're not going to suffer from the shock of retirement are we - going to work one day and having nothing to get up for the next?
>
> **John and Jackie Gunton b. 1945**

> I'm nearly 73 but I don't feel like an old man. The only thing that makes me feel old is when bits begin to crunch and creak. I realise I can't grip things as tight as I used to and I can't run now. My father died when he was 92. I've lived long enough to see a Labour Government and I hope I won't see another Conservative. The previous eighteen years politically were very depressing - the poll tax for instance ... I had to bite my tongue when I was in the police force - what the landed gentry around here say and do is considered to be what's right and what's wrong.
>
> **Richard Blythe b. 1926**

Some people I blame in a way for the world being polluted, not the older generation, but the middle-aged generation. The change from no cars on the road to lots of cars on the road is a bit difficult to understand and they don't know how to get it right.

Darren Fountain b. 1987

Getting older meant other people were getting the hassle:

When I was younger and I started growing my hair long the bulk of older people would keep you at arms length or take the Mickey - you were an outsider. You knew it and they knew it. These days people come to talk to me in the street easily - old ladies - young kids - it must just be the image I've got is a comfortable image to relate to. Up till I was about 27, I'd be stopped in the street because of the way I dressed. I'd sometimes walk barefoot - stopped by the police, searched for drugs, generally hassled. It stopped dead - about 1976/77. I realised I wasn't being stopped - I thought "hey - I look older". The police go for the kids because they're less developed, less responsible. Suddenly I was older. It was lovely not being hassled - then that developed further - people seemed to feel very comfortable with me. People don't look at me and look frightened or angry.

Squirrel b. 1951 ———

And the last word from Malcolm Booth:

I gave up cricket at the age of 64 - literally a sore point. I used to play for Alberbury and we always had a very good fixture with Oswestry. We were playing on a pitch which wasn't as good as usual. I was wearing glasses then and I didn't see a ball that suddenly reared and hit me, "Plonk!" I woke up in hospital at 10 o'clock at night with a very worried wife and elder son sitting beside my bed. The next morning a young Australian doctor came in and sat on the bed and said, "How old are you?" So I told him. And he said, "Don't you think it's time you took up umpiring?"

Malcolm Booth b. 1924

CHAPTER 9
TECHNOLOGY

Think back to the beginning of the century and imagine the
changes people have seen. It wasn't until recently you could
flick a switch and the room would light up - your water might
have come from the local well instead of a tap in the bathroom.
Now we have seen men in space and we can pick up the
telephone and dial Australia. How have people come to grips
with the changes in their lives? The labour saving devices.
How did they feel about using a telephone? Some confessed
to being true Luddites while others have jumped in at the
deep end and signed up on the Internet. Shropshire people
describe how technology has changed their lives.

Gordon Riley described his father's first radio:

> I'll never forget that radio coming into our house. It was called
> a Portadine. It had a wonderful piece of mechanism referred to
> as a moving coil - a little iron turntable. I used to hear it at six
> o'clock when father listened to the BBC news, and I listened to
> other programmes that he might like. It wasn't a case of leaving
> it on all the time. It was a battery operated radio - a so called
> portable - but it took two men and a butcher's boy to carry it
> round it was that heavy! It had the dry battery and the wet
> accumulator. I used to have to take the wet battery from
> Copthorne to what you will know as the Hartwell Garage
> opposite the Chronicle Offices which happened to be a garage
> then, combined with an undertakers. They had this system of
> charging up accumulators, it cost you 2d and you'd take one in
> and take another out.
>
> **Gordon Riley b. 1922**

Beryl Gower used her crystal set to learn tunes with a novel
way of amplification:

> You've heard of a crystal set? It's nick-name was 'the Cat's Whisker'.
> You could get two stations. There were five of us in the family and
> only two headphones - my father couldn't afford five headphones
> and of course we all wanted to listen so we put the headphones
> in a pudding basin and you could hear the voices quite clearly.
> It was like magic to me. If I was left for half an hour I'd use the
> headphones and I learnt a lot of the classical composers music
> from there. Then I'd go to the piano and play them.
>
> **Beryl Gower b. 1918**

*Dorothy Lutner remembered her first experience of
photography in Market Drayton:*

> We were waiting to have our photographs taken in the beautiful
> garden in the old Frog Lane we had in Market Drayton.
> A Mr Arnold, a new gentleman had come to open a photograph
> shop in the top of Stafford Street. He came along and he talked
> to us and put three large poles in the soft ground on top of
> which he had a little shelf and then a box. He covered it all over
> so there was just a little hole at the front and he told us to "smile!"
> Just two big clicks - and we didn't see how the photograph was
> taken and we were disappointed. I don't remember a flash.
> We stood very still. We were very good little girls.

Dorothy Lutner b. 1899

> My dad never used a telephone, and he only died three years
> ago. My mother used to have to go down to the telephone
> kiosk in Ketley if she wanted to make any calls, even in the
> 70s and 80s when I was away from home so much. Dad just
> regarded the telephone as an unnecessary item ... and I'm
> coming round to believing him. I've had to the live by the
> telephone and I've got three in this house, but it's still the
> device of the devil.
>
> ***You've just reminded me to turn my mobile off.***
>
> I've got one too. I'm in the trap like everybody else. I've got
> a separate phone for the internet on my computer, I've got
> a house phone and I've got a mobile.

Terry Lowe b. 1943

*Gordon Rose saw the benefit of technology for the
medical profession:*

> You've got to be able to move with the times. My secretaries
> you see - I introduced them to word processors but you can't
> do it straight away you have to do it in stages and they soon
> came to value them, but if I tried to introduce myself or my
> secretary to the internet I think we'd fail because we wouldn't
> feel in control.

Gordon Rose OBE b. 1916

Conversely, Gordon Riley felt the advent of new technology to the newsroom meant journalists lost their 'hands on' approach:

I feel sorry for the young journalists of today. Most of their time is spent on a computer, on the keyboard, on the telephone. I contrast it with my days as a cub reporter. My job was at the old Wellington Journal when its office was in Shoplatch. Journalism in my day? It was 90% sweat and meeting people and 5% luck. The telephone was in it's infancy and not a lot of people had it. You had to call on people, you had to meet people and had what I considered the great benefit of being able to see their eyes when you were talking to them. I didn't know the word at the time but I was able to judge their veracity when I was talking to them. On a news desk later I realised I was missing the eyes because I didn't have a yardstick to judge accurately the honesty of any statements being made to me over the telephone.

Gordon Riley b. 1922

I remember seeing my first aeroplane. It was wonderful to see one of those flying.

Edgar Gibbs b. 1908

Famous for gingerbread now Market Drayton was once the proud producer of a flying machine:

There opened in Old Bell Lane (now Queen's Street) the very first high class bicycle shop. When I was very small, the bicycle manufacturer, Mr Arthur Philips, was experimenting with aeroplanes, trying to make a machine that would fly. But he couldn't get anyone to work with him because they said it was the silliest thing they ever heard. But he did make it fly. All we little children went down to the cricket field in Market Drayton to see it go. There were quite a few people there and his machine, made with wires and with wings and a seat on it. It went up in the air and then came down again.

Was that the first time you saw anything leave the ground?

Oh, yes, that was the first time. There was something he wound up then it went straight up in the air and the people were surprised because they all thought he was mad. But it came down with a bump!

Dorothy Lutner b. 1899

95

Gordon Perks was working to install the first computers in a Shrewsbury factory:

It was all longhand, clerical work in the fifties. In the seventies we started to have a machine at our place and we'd start on punch cards. You'd mark them, then pass them to the punch card girl who'd feed them into the machine. In the machine was stored our stock and they'd take it off or put it on. It was like a computer. I worked for a long time with the computer planners. You'd decide on a system. Then you'd sit down with the computer planners and they'd interpret it in computer language. Then you'd hand it over to the computer people. It annoys me when I hear there's a mistake and people say its the computer again. It is never the computer.

Paranoia began to set in about computer technology leading to job losses:

The last system I was on we started to have VDUs in the early eighties. I was in an office and I was a leading hand of thirty odd, mostly girls. They feared for their jobs. We've had one computer and one operator and three jobs have gone. Some people took to the computer readily - some didn't. They feared it. I remember when we first had our telephone in we were frightened of it ringing because you could not see the person at the other end.

but Gordon was happy to take in all aspects:

I love my camcorder. The first one we had was all automatic. I had to have one. Anything - I spent two hours walking round the town with the floods. I can edit as much as I want to. I can put on a heading and I made up a good film of the golden wedding - and I've gone off still pictures.

Gordon Perks b. 1929

While Edgar Gibbs has embraced the microwave oven:

Oh yes I use the microwave ... Last Thursday it was the night for me to have my three ladies in playing bridge so I cooked a chicken ... baked a cake, I make a nice lemon sponge cake and I give them sandwiches and that.

Edgar Gibbs b. 1908

We've got the Internet now. It's fairly new but it could change the way everything is done. I mean money - in the future - we talk about having identity cards and people say we don't want that but it could be when we are born we are implanted

96

with a chip - you always would be you - you could walk through
a door and that could sense you - and if you're not allowed in
that door will not open. There might be no money ever again.

Squirrel b. 1951

Richard Beaumond found the Internet amazingly convenient:

I've recently bought a few CDs from Amazon on the Internet
and that's great because I didn't have to go to Shrewsbury!
I didn't have to drive to Shrewsbury, or queue up to get into
the place. I didn't have to walk to a store. At the end of a
computer terminal I could tap in a few numbers, press a few
buttons, and a couple of weeks later my CDs arrive. That's a
great benefit ... but where's it going to end? I'm afraid we might
be coming to a global version of having sold ourselves to the
company store. Whereby, yes, there will be choice on our
shelves but it will be a choice limited by what the manufacturers
and the owner of the manufacturing processes dictate.

Richard Beaumond b. 1948

And Judge Michael Mander's aunt nearly saw the moonshot:

I can still remember in the early fifties, when the first Russian
moon shot hit the moon, standing outside with my Great Aunt
who was then over eighty and a very devout woman looking
up at the full moon. We knew what time it was going to
happen. We watched and of course nothing happened.
She said, "There you are, I told you Michael, God would not
let it happen". I remember being amazed that it could happen.
The moon was 286,000 miles away and I was amazed that
anybody could fire a rocket at a moon and hit it as they proved
they did. And I felt humbled by my Great Aunt's faith and
bemused by her inability to take on board that this was happening.
What she would have made of people actually landing on the
moon - which she didn't survive to see - I don't know.

Judge Michael Mander b. 1936

*Shropshire is a rural county and while we get to grips with
the fax machine, the computer and the video - what's been
happening on the farm?*

I remember the last horse we had - I can't have been very big
because I remember going with my father to scuffle the weeds
out from between the swedes and the handles on the scuffle
which would have been waist height for an adult, I remember
having to reach up to them. That horse was called Snowdrop

and we sold her to the army and she became a drum horse, with a drum on each side for the army band. We've always been fond of horses. I like the attitude of Harold South, the late blacksmith in the village (he lived to be 96) I spent a lot of time with him. I asked him if he thought it would be nice to bring the horse back to agriculture and he said he was glad horse slavery had finished. I think that was probably a more accurate picture of horses on the farm than the romantic image we have now. I mean it's nice to see a horse doing a job on a short basis just to demonstrate how that job was done but when it had to be done day in and day out with a very early start to get up and feed the horses and a late start to put them to bed it was physically hard job for horse and man.

Jon Hayward b.1951

Margaret Oliver remembers the start of mechanisation:

I can remember the poor horses being confused when the first tractor arrived. It was a spud wheel tractor because we were on fairly heavy land and they didn't have these great heavy tyres they have these days. We still kept the horses because they were useful for lugging in the hay and straw.

Margaret Oliver b. 1929

Robert Read-Griffiths returned to the family farm in 1977 after taking a degree in agricultural engineering:

The big changes in technology had already arrived before me, the combine harvester, the milking machine and no great change has happened in the thirty years I've been running the farm. Only the degree.

So father was already switched on was he?

Oh yes. We moved into making silage rather than making hay. That was perhaps the impetus of the younger generation moving on. It was much less stressful.

Robert Read-Griffiths b. 1955

Don Stokes was ahead of his time:

When I was in Canada in 1947 I was given the name of the man who was reputedly the best dairy farmer in Canada. So I went to see him in Vancouver. His dairy herd was so outstanding it was almost unbelievable. His herd average was three times the British output. He had a Swiss herdsman who lived actually above the cows. This herdsman came down in the middle of the night and gave the animals an extra feed; one just before midnight and one at four o'clock in the morning. I thought, "Gosh! Has this man found the key to very, very high production?" A few years later, in the early 1950s I heard a radio programme which talked about the invention of a transponder. All of a sudden it came to me. By Jove! If I could fit a transponder onto a cow and make a machine that switched itself on when the transponder came near it, a cow could help itself to the feed. You wouldn't have to get up at night to feed them. If a cow wanted a feed it could go to the machine. So I drew a rough sketch of the machine that I thought would accommodate this and went over to our local manufacturers. They made a prototype which was so successful they patented it and went into production. Unfortunately the patents weren't quite as water-tight as they should have been and within three years there were thirteen other competitors making a similar type of thing. But I was paid a royalty on the invention and it has worked extremely well.

So how exactly does it work?

The cow has a chain around its neck and on it is this little electronic gadget. When it goes up to the feed dispenser the transponder gets near to a receiver which gets a message to discharge so much feed for the cow. How much the cow gets each time and how many feeds it has per day are in the control of the farmer. The cow can be allocated four or six extra feeds a day, but she can't get more than her allocation so she doesn't become sick by over-eating. She has a small amount - and often - which enables the cow to produce this really quite remarkable amount of milk.

And the cowman gets a good night's sleep?

Yes. Everybody's happy!

Don Stokes b. 1923 ————

Don was using the latest farming technology as well as inventing it:

When we had the binder, farm labour was very cheap and all through the war we'd used prisoners of war here at Houghton Farm to help with the harvest. After the war, people became more expensive to employ. I had seen this advanced system of combined harvesting in the United States and so in the early 1950s I bought the first combined harvester here which was a small and rather insignificant machine which bagged all the grain up. It wasn't as combined a harvester as we have today but it did completely save farm labour. The threshing days disappeared and the harvest took only a twentieth of the time it used to.

What happened to the men your combined harvester replaced?

The government at the time was very keen on full employment and the loss of equipment and appliances during the war meant that factories could almost work night and day trying to fulfil the demand for this country and for export. So the demand for factory labour was very high. Just after the war for example we employed six people. Three years later two of them had got jobs in factories and another joined the railways who were also looking for manpower. So there was this gradual diminution in labour. I don't think I ever gave a man the sack. Every single one of them thought they'd go to pastures new, away from Ellesmere, and get more pay.

And the last word from Don Stokes about the milking parlour he still uses today:

In 1938 when we came here we milked by hand. We had six milkers, including two women who came from Ellesmere, to help us milk morning and night. In the middle 1940s we used milking machines and a cowshed. This went on for fifteen years when the milking parlour came into vogue. But then in spring 1970 we had a prototype Rotary Parlour installed. It was the first of its kind in the UK, created by Fullwood of Ellesmere. We had something like three thousand visitors coming to see it from all over the world, including Japan. They'd stand eight at a time in a viewing room, looking through one-way glass so the cows wouldn't be distracted.

How does the machine work?

The cows enter the rotary parlour and go round, like a merry-go-round, in a mechanised cow cell. The one man milking them stands in one position and the cows come in, get fed, are milked and go round and then off.

Do the cows enjoy it?

Absolutely, yes! You've only got to see how keen they are to get onto it.

Don Stokes b. 1923

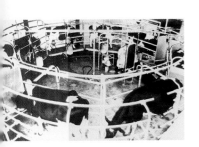

CHAPTER 10
EATING & DRINKING

What we eat and drink, how we cook, where we buy our food has changed beyond recognition from the beginning of the century to the end. The availability of different produce from the supermarket shelves and the onset of convenience food all comes under scrutiny. How many people in the 1990s keep a pig at the bottom of the garden? What was available to eat during rationing? Have the supermarkets changed our lives for the better? Are we going to embrace the concept of GM (Genetically Modified) foods? Or will there be a backlash against them? Is cookery really the new "rock and roll"? Are food scares the stuff of the 1990s? Shropshire people share their thoughts, views and feelings - and a few recipes - in the changes of our eating habits over the century.

Shopping for food was a different concept and Alf Cheadle remembers his mother's grocery shop doubling as a fish and chip shop once a week:

Mother's shop in Bomere Heath was just a little room really, but it sold everything. Zubes, De Witts, bacon, pills, cigarettes, coconut matting, wellington boots - all general groceries. She also did fish and chips which was quite common in the rural areas in the thirties. I had a bicycle with a home-made trailer. I used to go down to meet the milk train at Leaton Station on Tuesday mornings and collect the fresh fish which arrived in boxes strapped with wire and covered in ice. I'd bring it back home and then go to school. Nobody would sit next to me at school on a Tuesday. My mother meanwhile would fillet and cut up the fish and boil and dress the crabs and then take it all out in a basket to walk round the village selling it to her clients. And I'd come home from school, get on my bike and go round the outlying districts selling the fish there. Then in the evening my mother would do fish and chips in our kitchen on a domestic range with a big vat of fat ... people would come to the back door to buy it. The front door was the grocer's shop, the back door was the fish and chip shop. It was 3d for a fish, 1d for the chips and we did squashy peas as well.

Alf Cheadle b. 1922

Evelyn Hatton uses her memories of rationing as a basic shopping list:

> When I'm shopping even now, I always go through the rations. When I lived in Pontesbury, that's the sort of things you'd buy, butter, marge, cheese, lard, sugar, tea, bacon, eggs - I always go through the rations, it was instilled into you - soap powder and things like that. But it was funny in those days. They packed up your order in a box, but you had to pay for the box, 3d it was. I shop in Sainsbury's in Oswestry now, you can't compare them. I enjoy going but in the old days it was completely different - then the customers were always right.
>
> **Evelyn Hatton b. 1926**

Elaine Bruce looked back on the early days of the supermarket:

> I thought the advent of the supermarket was wonderful.
> I was very naive. I thought they were doing a great service and it was very handy to go and fill a trolley once a month. I still used a local butcher and a local greengrocer. Things like fresh dairy produce, fresh meat, fresh vegetables I would get from the specialist small shops. It never occurred to me to get those from the supermarket in those early days.
>
> **Elaine Bruce b. 1938**

A different concept of shopping from the old days:

> Mother was wonderful, she'd stop down at Oakengates Market until it was 10 o'clock at night and things were cheap. We had beautiful meals because she paid hardly anything for it - sometimes they gave it away.
>
> **Iris Butler b. 1919**

Or catching your own:

> In those days we lived on rabbits, roast, stewed. Father used to have a shotgun. He used to take us up the back. Up the fields to a farm called Malt Hall. It's still there. There was a big pit mound there, with some brambles at the bottom. He used to stand on the mound and we used to beat the brambles and the rabbits ran up the mound to him and bang! That's how we got a lot of our food. We used to grow a lot. The rabbits had shotgun pellets in them and as you were eating them you had to spit them out. Even now I would eat a rabbit. We kept chickens. When we went to the toilet up at the top of the garden the cockerel would let you in but he wouldn't let you

out. He used to fly at you. We kept goats, ducks, and there was a brook running by the side of the house with quite a lot of trout in. We put out night lines with a bent pin and caught trout in a bucket. You would see a trout by the bank, get underneath it and very gently they'd allow you to tickle their belly with your fingers and they loved it. Gradually you'd move your fingers up to their gills and you'd push two hands in their gills and pull them out. We caught eels and we'd take them into dad and he'd reward us with a sweet or maybe a marble.

Gordon Perks b. 1929

> **Mother made a lot of this home made jam. Not like this bought'un tack. It was lovely!**
>
> **Dennis Crowther b. 1926**

Butcher Edgar Gibbs talked about the days before refrigeration:

Tell me about your first shop.

We used to hang some of the meat outside in the early days ... outside the entrance ... of course there wasn't all the fumes and all the things we get now. We hadn't got refrigeration. They used to come along from the factory up at Meole Brace and bring you a block of ice, we had what they call an ice box down in the basement. We broke the ice up and put salt with it. In the very hot weather we used to cut the orders on Thursday and in the ice factory at Meole Brace you could rent a place to keep your orders.

Edgar Gibbs b. 1908 ────

I can remember walking up the Cop in Shrewsbury and seeing whole sides of beef hanging outside Davies the Butchers. He'd come out of the shop, hack a piece off and there'd be blue-bottles floating about. The fishmongers on the Cop had a great big open slab of fish.

Marie Kelly b. 1914

Flower Show days in Shrewsbury were a busy time at Edgar's butcher's shop:

All the people coming to the Flower Show used to come by train and walk up Castle Gates, thousands of them - you could almost walk on their heads at times. We used to make pork pies and when they came back they'd buy a pork pie and take it back with them to Lancashire or South Wales. The smallest was 1lb in weight. We made just over a thousand pies for the two days of the show.

Edgar Gibbs b. 1908

Betty Toon became a hotelier in Shrewsbury after the War. The meals there were a varied selection but the inspector must have thought they lived on macaroni cheese:

We bought the (now demolished) Beauchamps Hotel on The Mount in Shrewsbury in November 1947. Rationing went on until '54 or '55 and our meat ration for the whole of the hotel for one week would be one leg of lamb. So every time the AA inspector came to the hotel the only thing we'd got to feed him was macaroni cheese. It happened time after time! Also, interestingly, well into the late 50s the only thing you could serve was meat, mashed potato and peas. The change in eating habits has been incredible since then. The turning point was in the late 60s when a wider range of vegetables was introduced, but we still had to stick to meat and two veg. The advent of the deep freeze made a considerable difference as we grew a lot of our own vegetables. Also the hotel kept bees and we produced enough honey for the breakfast tables throughout the year. We had a very good black market cupboard, I might tell you! Otherwise we wouldn't have got by. Local farmers had surplus produce and local fishermen would come to the back door with a salmon. You just hoped the AA inspector came round on a macaroni cheese day!

Betty Toon b. 1919

but the supermarket was eventually going to hold sway:

It never entered my head that a supermarket meat counter could possibly compete with a local butcher.
Elaine Bruce b. 1938

There is still controversy in Ludlow:

We don't need another supermarket in Ludlow. We've got two which appeal to different ends of the economic range in the town. That's enough. If people want large supermarkets and they've got their cars you're not going to stop them going to other places anyway - and a middling sized supermarket - which is all the site can afford in Ludlow isn't going to compete. When a large supermarket comes to a small country town it only takes two or three years for the small specialist shops to vanish.

Elaine Bruce b. 1936

Shops have evolved to suit people's demands. Two years ago Sunday shopping was illegal. Now its one of the biggest shopping days of the week. Things don't go back.
Alex Williams b. 1933

*New traditions began to evolve and the variety of food
increased to cater for different tastes and new Salopians'
requirements:*

Nowadays people are coming over from Wolverhampton.
There are Indian shops and you can get all sorts of things.
Things are starting to get better with food, now you can get
green banana, yam, sweet potato so gradually everything just
becomes normal. Indians have started to come with vans from
Wolverhampton - they bring really good things, so we're well
away now with West Indian food. Gradually we've started to
get things in tins but I don't like tinned things. I'd rather have
fresh ones. So now you just get things like you're back home.
I don't miss Jamaica now for food.

Vicky Cowell b. 1931

I was brought up on beer.

Bill Caddick b. 1944

*The Japanese community soon established which shops
would cater for their needs:*

To get good seafood for Japanese recipes we have to go to the
fish market in Birmingham. We use very thin sliced meat which
you British people don't use. Fortunately in Much Wenlock
there is a butcher who will do that especially for Japanese
people. So most Japanese housewives go to him.

Noaki Midori b. 1965

Alternative methods of shopping are also beginning to emerge:

We first started selling produce on the WI stall in the market at
Whitchurch. It was Jackie's idea ... we needed somewhere where
we could sell small quantities without having to pay a full market
rate and it had to be a regular outlet, we didn't want to take stuff
to a shop and have them say yes we love it one week and not
want it the next. It's a brilliant organisation. The WI market stalls
are separate from the local groups. You buy a share and then
you have to abide by their rules for packing things and take a
turn on the stall occasionally. You pay a commission for handling.
There's a wide range of products you can buy.

John and Jackie Gunton b. 1945

The latest thing we've got in Ludlow is the most fantastic
box scheme - you know an organic fruit and vegetable box -
that started about four years ago as quite a small scheme -

now it's operating all over Shropshire. How does it work? Well you subscribe - you might want a £5 a week fruit box or a £10 a week vegetable box or whatever. You 'phone your order through then go to a local pick up point to collect your order and pay for it. The contents are all organic.

Elaine Bruce b. 1936

In a rural county like Shropshire it was perhaps more traditional in the past to 'grow your own'. Alex Williams from T & O Williams in Wem still managed to keep on the ice cream even during the war:

During the war you weren't allowed to have milk for ice cream but if you had goats you could use goat's milk. There was a chap in Wem with two goats in his backyard and I thank God those goats kept going all through the war! They fed Wem with ice cream - and the most delicious ice cream throughout the war.

Alex Williams b. 1933

Market Drayton was the food capital of Shropshire:

Most of the groceries we used to have came from Drayton. There was Braznell Smith and Cushings. Braznell Smith used to come early in the week, take the order and deliver bits and pieces. There is still a shop in the square which I think is still called Cushings, but it's changed. That was the higher class one. Braznell Smith was the grocers. It was wooden floor with high counters, rather gloomy. High shelves and little cubby holes. I'm not sure how they kept the butter there but I expect it was all patted up into shapes and things. The grains were in boxes and cupboards.

Margaret Oliver b. 1929

It wasn't always a rural idyll on the farm:

When they bled the pig you got a bucketfull of blood and you had to stir the blood by hand and keep stirring till you got all the clots out of it. You kept your fingers open to collect the clots, and I was nearly up to my elbow in blood and I hated it. It was a horrible job, but you did it because it had to be done.

Ernest Griffiths b. 1920

There was plenty of community spirit and people would kill pigs in rotation and share the meat around:

Piglets would be born and after about twelve weeks, cut and weaned. Sterilised you see. People would perhaps buy a couple. In my grandmother's day they'd have to buy two pigs and sell one to buy the salt to cure the other with. Because salt was that scarce.

How long would the pig be in the sty for?

It would be from about August or September up until nearly Christmas. The pig then would be 12 or 13 scores in weight. (There was 20 pounds in a score) It was slaughtered so there was a good supply of food for Christmas. The bacon would not be too fat or big, just a manageable size. The women of the house undertook everything regarding the pig. The day it was slaughtered the liver and lungs would be taken out and distributed among the neighbours because it wouldn't keep. They'd take the ribs out and the backbone - which they always called the "chine". The pig's head was cut off and the sides of bacon and hams cured in a big vat called a "cooler". They'd rub saltpetre on the joints or the parts where there was any residue of blood. We children would use the left over saltpetre to make invisible ink. Then we helped with cutting up the fat from around the kidney and that would be rendered down into lard. Spare ribs would be sent to relatives perhaps all over the country. The local postman would be inundated with parcels because you could always guarantee that if you posted a rib one day it would get anywhere in the British Isles the next day ... still fresh when it arrived.

Emily Griffiths b. 1917

Fruit picking was a way of augmenting the income and Emily Griffiths described the bilberry harvest:

I was carried onto the hills to pick bilberries before I could walk and I was adept at picking. I'd be sat down with a little cup in what we called a "plack", which was a little patch. With my little fingers I would pick the bilberries and they would be emptied into a big basket carried by my mother. Those were the financial life-line for the people of that area. They only earned a small wage and the bilberry picking came once a year. The earliest I recall picking bilberries was 27th June and the latest I've ever picked edible bilberries from the hills was 6th November. That's a long period. But the school holidays of six weeks always coincided with the ripening of the bilberry crop. Children would pick from morning till night. In those days they were taken mainly for the dye works ...

they were not eaten as they are now. They were picked by
the quart or the pint - measured, not weighed - and the
horse and cart would come to a given point. People would
come rushing down off the hills with their bilberries to have
them measured and they might be paid 3 ha'pence a quart.
But that money perhaps bought a pig to fatten up for the
winter, new shoes for the children to go back to school after
the summer holidays, and perhaps something in the way of
new clothing. The best year was after the bad winter of 1947.
That year I picked twenty eight and a half pounds in one day.
You couldn't put your foot down for them - they covered
everywhere. An old country-wise gentleman who lived in the
area would say, "If you want to know where the best bilberries
will be, you watch where the snow lies the longest." True!

Emily Griffiths b. 1917

**Vegetarians and vegans had an unfortunate tendency
in those days to say [of BSE] "well, you should have
listened to us in the first place"**

Elaine Bruce b. 1938

Vicky Cowell's religion prompted her choice of diet:

I don't buy chips because in our church you have to be careful
what you eat because we don't do anything with animal fat.
I would prefer to buy oven chips but not from the fish and chip
shop because you don't know what sort of animal fat they use.
Don't get me wrong - I eat what the English cook but I don't
eat any meat if I go anywhere. I have greens or fish, things like
this. I go to a church that is a vegetarian church.

Vicky Cowell b. 1931

**We have so many fads in food. I looked at something
this morning and it said 95% fat free. Before it would
have said 5% fat but 95% fat free sounds so much better.**

Alex Williams b. 1933

*Terry Tandler likes the link with tradition brewing his
own cider gives:*

I'm carrying on a tradition. If you want some good cider you've
got to make it yourself - you can get some good stuff - Dunkertons
- one or two of the small brews - but this designer stuff is terrible.
I like a drink of cider - especially when I'm gardening. Nothing better
than when it's April, May, and you've dug a good plot of garden
for the taters and then about 9 o'clock going up to the shed and

getting yourself a mug of cider to drink when it's just getting dusk. You've done all the work towards it and you haven't paid a penny for it and it tastes all the nicer. You've put all the effort. You can't make it decently without proper cider fruit. Some are sharp and acid, some are sweet and juicy, but you've got to have a balance of acid and tannin, if there's no tannin the cider won't keep - and you've got to have plenty of juice and the sugar content within it. If you just use cookers or eaters it just won't make cider.

Terry Tandler b. 1951 ———

In Jamaica we used fresh food, I'd never eaten frozen food. In Jamaica you have a garden round your home with greens, carrots, callaloo, spinach ... callaloo is like spinach but the leaves are a bit smaller. It has a lot of iron in it just like spinach. We mostly steam it with saltfish.

Vicky Cowell b. 1931

Looking back it appears food scares were not just a thing of the 1990s

When we had the foot and mouth disease ... the first one I remember was in the mid 1920s... some people were put off meat because of them being slaughtered.

Edgar Gibbs b.1908

Scrapie in sheep was also a problem when he was a boy as Edgar Gibbs describes:

I can remember one of the workmen knocking on the door one morning and saying, "Gaffer, there's a sheep gone down the gib..." I went down with him and he took his knife and slaughtered it ... I remember him splitting the head open and the brain was practically all liquid.

Edgar Gibbs b. 1908 ———

Concern over the food we eat continued through the generations:

I'm not sure which is worse: the idea of feeding creatures on other creatures or producing tomatoes in tomato puree or grain with bits of genes from pigs or viruses. I find the two ideas equally repellent. They're like science fiction.

Elaine Bruce b. 1938

And it seems the public have been rather more sceptical about genetically modifying food than expected:

Nature is the biggest modifier of genetics there is, within any population there is a mutation rate ... you can observe the mutation rate in bacteria ... all sorts of things in nature cause mutations and in nature only the favourable survive ... we would have no evolution without mutation ... everybody catches onto the fish gene in tomatoes, it didn't work but the fact that it was done once is enough to create Frankenstein crop issues and media scares.

Wilson Boardman b. 1955

It's very heartening they have caught onto that because it is the most serious threat to our possible future health and people are beginning to be outraged that they have callously and cynically been made into guinea pigs for an experiment the end of which no-one knows. Some countries have banned it altogether.

Elaine Bruce b. 1938

and interest in organic produce is growing apace:

There's more interest in our stuff than there was. People are not only keen on organic produce but on locally grown produce. The locally grown thing is probably bigger than the organic - its fresh. There is a general suspicion of the big multinationals

John Gunton b. 1945

or perhaps it was there all along:

After the war we didn't want anything to do with white sliced bread. We still wanted to make the old fashioned proper loaf. At the time there was a chap called Sam Mayall from Harmer Hill who had certain principles (they called him a nutter in London) and he wanted to have his place free of all chemicals (DDT and so on) and so he was organic long before the word organic existed and we made his bread, Pimhill bread. We still make it.

Alex Williams b. 1933

I don't use any chemicals. This comes from that time when there was a disillusionment with science. I was trained as a scientist and I was as disillusioned as everyone. Nature needs to be treated with respect and care.

John Gunton b. 1945

Changes in farming methods meant a changing environment for Shropshire beekeeper, John Oliver:

We don't get anything like the honey we used to. I've got photos of Margaret standing beside a hive bigger than she was. This is partly because of the herbicides. A lot of forage is killed off. You don't see fields of grain with poppies and other flowers in them - you just see the grain - so that forage is gone. There has been trouble with insecticide.

You were involved in getting the legislation changed?

I was chairman of the Beekeeping Association at the time so I was in the thick of it. We had a case of some aerial spraying where they were going way out from the crop. It particularly happened with a friend of mine out at Shrawardine. They were on one side of the river and the farmer had something sprayed the other side and they lost all their bees. We kicked up a shindig. We didn't get any sense from the Ministry of Agriculture. They didn't want to know. We didn't get much help from the British Beekeepers Association. What happened in the end was we took it up with the Minister of Aviation. He was very sympathetic and actually wrote to me and said there is no case law in this country for suing the operators or the farmer but he did quote New Zealand and Australian cases for me which I thought was pretty good going. The furore that we created! The regulations that covered aerial spraying were tightened up - so it was quite nice to have actually done something. I went to see two MPs, but you were just banging your head against a brick wall. Beekeepers are a very insignificant minority. The one thing that did cause them to flutter was when we said we're not doing any more pollination contacts. Now there's not much goes on in this area but it did put the fear of God into them! We were very lucky with [local reporters]. They took it up and it was in the national newspapers every week, trotting out the whole story - and it was on the television.

John & Margaret Oliver b. 1929 ────

The penultimate word from Alex Williams:

During the war you did not leave anything on your plate, you ate it all, like it or lump it.

And he should know what he's talking about:

I was chairman of the Shropshire grocers association. I remember the first time I judged cheese, here at Wem show. It was only Cheshire in those days. There were three classes - coloured, white and novice and my fellow judge - Nellie Benyon, said to me," You find the supreme champion". I said, "but I'm only the student judge" but she said "Go on." So I went round and came back a bit shamefaced. I said, "I've given it to the novice", and she said, "So you should, it was the best cheese".

Alex Williams b. 1933

111

CHAPTER 11
MONEY

*Living with it and living without it. The English reticence about
discussing it. The frightening poverty at the beginning of the
century and the ability of the people to cope and make the
best of things with very little. In these discussions the people
of Shropshire talk about their feelings on the subject of money
and their perceptions about the wealth and poverty of the past,
the present and the future.*

Somedays I think my God - what have I done with my life?
I should have got that piece of paper, that job and that pension
scheme - but I now still have the freedom to be a millionaire
tomorrow. There's no ceiling on my income, no limit of
possibility. Potentially I'm free to become secure.

Squirrel b. 1951

We'd got no money worries because we hadn't got none.
Dennis Crowther b. 1926

Sometimes help can come from mysterious sources:

I remember one experience a few years ago which shook me.
My wife was going into hospital for a hip replacement.
Naturally I was concerned, but I was not worried. I felt this
tremendous consciousness of God's presence. It was the most
wonderful experience of my life. I was looking out of the
window and I saw the whole of nature transformed then He
gave me a sign, "before you call I will answer". This was the
proof. Because it was urgent I had sent Winnie to the Nuffield
for her operation and was paying for it privately. Operations are
pretty expensive. That morning I received two cheques one for
£1000 and one for £750. I was going to fetch her home that
morning. When I went to the Nuffield and sat down to make
out the cheque the Bursar said, "Before you make out the cheque,
Vicar I have some good news for you. Somebody (who wished
to be anonymous) has paid the first £1000 of your bill."
I was amazed and I was obviously very deeply moved.

The Reverend John Ayling b. 1902

*Shopping at the local supermarket could never have been
like Evelyn's description of the system at the village stores:*

When you went down to the shop, I always went every day, people
didn't pay every day. It wasn't the sort of shop where there wasn't

any credit. We had a day book and people came in for things they wanted and they were put down in the day book. The next morning I used to have to write those on their bills. The farmers in the country, they didn't pay every time, they had monthly statements. People were very good payers. You got the odd one or two of course - the people that had got the most were the worst payers.

Evelyn Hatton b. 1926

Unsettled times in the 1920s meant careful assessments were needed:

My father had made money in the early 1920s in the skin trade, which had gone up. And then when it came down it was a rather funny period because you never knew who was going to go up the spout (if you've heard that expression). You needed to get information from London about what was happening, who'd gone bankrupt, what prices were falling and information got here by telegram. The telegraph boy would come and I knew I had to read it and say, "No answer", because the boy was waiting for an answer. These warned my father who not to send stock to.

Mary Hignett b. 1912

Times changed for the clergy, too:

We were as poor as our poorest parishioners until we came to Myddle. I was getting about £2000 a year in 1959. Now a man gets a wonderful modern vicarage rent free, rates free, with all his repairs paid for, all the expenses paid and about £15,000 a year - and his wife goes to work. Wives weren't allowed to go to work then. They were gentry wives. They had to work in the parish.

The Reverend John Ayling b. 1902

It was hard to bring up seven children on the wages of the time but unemployment meant poverty and resorting to unconventional methods:

There was an accident and my father was classed as unfit to go down the pit ... that was a terrible blow because we were very short of money. In those days you only got proper unemployment pay for twelve months and then you went onto a thing called the Means Test. They came round your house and if you'd got anything worth selling you had to sell it ... that's when he started poaching.

Della Bailey b. 1928

Most people grew their own vegetables as matter of course:

We didn't have a lot of money, but we always had quite enough to live on. Father made sure we were all as well educated as we could be. That was very important to him - to both of them. We had a long garden in Meole which was cultivated and he had another garden down on the Lower Road, one of the houses in Meole (the houses were one side of the road, the gardens another) which went down to the brook. He produced his own produce - as we do still. We go out into the garden and get what we want. We're not entirely self sufficient. I don't think we were then either.

John Oliver b. 1929

I think bringing in the lottery system has caused enormous problems. It's the wonderful thrill of the gambling instinct - I might be one of the lucky ones - I might win all that money. On the other hand a great deal of the lottery money has gone to good causes and it's been wonderful for the country. It's very hard - you're split in two.

Beryl Gower b. 1918

Farm wages are good now for full time craftsmen - £240 isn't to be sneezed at. You've got good clean air to breathe out here in the country.

Fred Jordan b. 1922

Moving to Shropshire from Jamaica in the 1950s meant a re-assessment of finances:

I didn't take long to get a job at Sankey. My husband worked there. When I came here first he was working at a place called Walcot, but he was only getting £7 a week and we had to pay £5 a week rent. But things were cheap in those days ... in Wellington you could get your whole week's shopping for £2, not of the best, nothing too expensive. You just have to live off what you could.

Vicky Cowell b. 1931

Self sufficiency, it seems, will never make people wealthy - at least not in monetary terms:

The market stall we have is our only income. We've been here 22 years - the only money we earned, virtually our entire income, is from the market garden. Beyond that we've only earned £300 between us.

John and Jackie Gunton b. 1945

Of course, things were cheaper then:

> The grandfather clock in the corner I bought for £12.10 in
> the old market hall. I'd see something I liked on a Tuesday
> and my mother would go down on the Wednesday and bid
> for it and it would come back to our home in Oak Street on
> the back of a horse and cart. I got a set of Clun Chairs for
> about £5. They're straight backed chairs with a wooden seat
> and a carved back.

Named after the Clun in Shropshire?

> Yes, if you go down to that part of the world you can find
> them. We saw some in Bishop's Castle the other week. It's
> quite staggering we bought these for so little.

John Oliver b. 1929

*Times were hard even for those who were lucky enough to
find permanent employment:*

> My father volunteered for the great war and spent the
> greater part in France with the KSLI and when he came
> back to the world fit for heroes to live in he was unemployed
> for a very long time. He eventually got a job with the local
> council tar spraying, but that disappeared - it was seasonal -
> but luckily he got a job on the railway and eventually became
> permanent. I know in 1932 his wages were 22/- a week.
> At that time I was 11 years old. So keeping mother and son
> was difficult but although I didn't have everything I wanted I
> had everything I needed through great sacrifices on the part
> of my parents.

Gordon Riley b. 1922

And harder still for those who hadn't:

> There was appalling poverty in Shropshire in the thirties.
> The old people would talk about it. For instance, there was
> a couple living under the A5 in an archway. They just had a
> horse and cart to do a bit of rag and bone work. That's
> appalling poverty isn't it to strike an area like this? Kids
> wouldn't go to school because they hadn't got the clothes ...
> and mother would have to buy an army blanket to make
> them a suit and then the child's legs would be rubbed raw
> by the rough cloth in the cold weather. There was real
> poverty in the thirties around what we now call Telford.

Cath Marshall b. 1920

There was a fund run by the Shrewsbury Borough Police force for needy children. They provided boots and shoes so they could go to school well shod. There was a sense of status that they were poor children and people didn't like being classed as poor in those days.

Gordon Riley b. 1922

I think my parents passed on that you have to work to get what you want. I wouldn't say I was a workaholic but I think my sister is. She lives for work. She works with mentally and physically handicapped children. I would think she derives a lot of pleasure from that ... but I don't think she gets paid her just reward for the hours that she puts in ... whereas I'm probably in the position that I get my just reward, in fact, probably more than my just reward for the hours that I put in.

Dave Smart b. 1958

You're treated differently, often on how much money you have, how well you're dressed. The idea that Britain is getting to be a classless society - I don't see that.

Jackie Gunton b. 1945

When my mother died in 1972, I became a much more permanent fixture at Linley Hall because at that stage I had no proper home to go to. I spent my holidays up here and I worked on the farm to earn pocket money. I was completely incompetent.

Justin Coldwell b. 1953

I was very nearly 22 before I got £1 a week, living in. Farm wages weren't good.

Fred Jordan b. 1922

I could have gone to the Priory School but we couldn't afford the uniform.

Muriel Painter b. 1925

Emma Bullock describes the poverty in other areas:

When I lived in Birkenhead before the war the poverty was dreadful, children, some of them never had a pair of shoes, they were so cold and ill clad and they looked so waxen because they were hungry. We used to have a big Christmas breakfast for a thousand of them. Some of them used to put pie in their pockets to take for the others. I never saw a child like that in Shrewsbury.

Emma Bullock b. 1911

117

There is still an innate wariness of credit:

One of the greatest changes this century has been the introduction of plastic money. My father could have bought his house for £400. Now that same row of houses is selling for a quarter of a million. But dad wouldn't buy it at the time because he didn't want to get into debt. As I don't want to now. I've got no credit cards or anything like that. I'll pay cash every time and save up for what I want. Now this is a big change over the last forty years. People before the war did not want to involve themselves in debt. They might take out a mortgage but that would be their only debt. But a couple can meet and get married and be in a house and in debt in a fortnight now. All these credits cards are a ruination of so many happy marriages. People get into debt and cannot clear their debts.

Alan J Gardner b. 1912

In Broseley the introduction of the Credit Union bank has helped:

I've been working very hard to make people understand the concept and to accept that it is right and useful to them. There was one particular lady who was a very key person in the community who for nine months had been watching what we were doing. I've known her and we've disagreed over issues quite strongly and then she suddenly came to me and said, "I want to join that. I've watched you and if somebody's going to do that for nine months without being paid and it's helping all these people then I'm going to be part of it".

Jo Havell b. 1943

> **Nothing came into our house that wasn't paid for.**
> **Della Bailey b. 1928**

Getting into debt was, and still is a frightening prospect. Jo Havell hoped her venture with the Credit Union will prevent stories like this from happening in the future:

One particular incident made it very clear to me that there was a role for the Credit Union. A person got behind with certain payments and tried to forget it, put it on one side, had in fact got the bailiffs involved and suddenly from owing a very small amount, owed hundreds of pounds. The point of intervention should have been when the small amount was owing. She needed advice and she needed support but she also needed a small amount of money. With the Credit Union - that could have been the resolution point.

Jo Havell b. 1943

Terry Tandler's rural background provided him with an analogy:

I get fed up with the monetarists saying we've only had half a per cent growth - we need 5,6,10 per cent growth in the economy. You look at an oak tree. It grows for 200 - 300 years and it gets to it's maximum size and then it stays at that level, if it's left for the next 500 or 600 hundred years - if it's left. What would happen if it grew its branches longer and longer? They'd snap off. You could say that's what's happening in the economy, in the modern civilisation. Instead of growing to a maximum size and then staying actively alive at that size it has to keep growing until branches bust off and then disease gets in.

Terry Tandler b. 1951 ———

Old habits die hard:

I'm better off money-wise than I've ever been in my life. But I'm very careful. I never want to spend it because I always think I might need it. And the children keep saying to me, "Mum don't be so silly. There's been times when you haven't had it but now you have. Spend it on yourself." But I've got that feeling that I ought not to spend it. I can't help it.

Nellie Rowson b. 1914

and sometimes those who have the wherewithal like to keep it!

Father hated to be in debt. That's why the mortgage he took out was a very limited one and was fairly quickly paid off. He couldn't have got a car except by hire purchase and he didn't want to go down that road. He was very critical of people who couldn't pay their bills or resorted to tick, and would sometimes talk a little indiscreetly perhaps to my mother with me there, and would mention names. He would say things like, "Isn't it awful. They strut around the town as if they own the place but they owe me so many pounds and I can't get it out of them." My mother would then say to me, "You shouldn't have heard that David. You mustn't mention that to anyone." But this appalled him. His perception was that people who cut a fine dash in society, as it were, were often those who didn't pay their bills.

David Lloyd b. 1935

CHAPTER 12

PLAYTIME

From the Olympic Games to Australian cricket, dancing to hop scotch, film clubs to strip joints , Shropshire people reveal how they keep themselves amused in their leisure time. We hear the backstage gossip from Ludlow Festival and tales of Hollywood, disillusionment with the current TV programmes and from the lady who has spent 50 years disrupting the 'Sport of Kings'.

John Oliver's fascination with bees and bee keeping began after he left the army:

> It was after I came out of the army and I settled down I suddenly decided I'd keep bees. I read some books about it and I got in touch with Brian Pearce who was then secretary of the local beekeepers association. He said come out and see me and we'll go through a hive and have a look at it. I got stung while I was there and he said he arranged that on purpose because so many people think they are going to keep bees and as soon as they have a sting or two they decide not. You're bound to get that. Nowadays I don't really notice it. I don't know what the magic is. It's a whole form of different life.
>
> **John Oliver b. 1929**

John Oliver used his cine camera to record an amazing film of drumming bees from one skep to another:

> We both had an interest in theatre and films. I had visions of being a film director. I was brought up on Eisenstein. We used to go to the film society in Attingham, see all the foreign films. I got hold of a cine camera and I decided to make a film on driving bees. In the old days of skep beekeeping you couldn't take a frame out of the thing because the combs were built into the straw skeps. The way you collected your honey was to turn the skep upside down, put an empty skep on the top at an angle of about 45 degrees, put two pins holding it together and there were some driving irons you put in it to keep the things apart. You drummed the bottom one with your fingers and the bees become mesmerised and start walking up into the empty skep. When the queen goes up there's a mad rush and they all go and you end up with the empty skep - apart from the eggs and the brood, so you loose all the brood. Then you take it all apart, put the bees back on their stand, with a stick under the corner to hold the skep up. I thought it would be nice to record it.
>
> **John Oliver b. 1929**

Gordon Perks mixed with some illustrious company when he was in the Navy:

I used to play hockey with the Duke of Edinburgh in Malta. He was out there. He was a real tough guy. I'd rather play in the same team as him than against him. I got to know him pretty well. When he was on board ship he was a very strict officer but when he was out playing hockey he was really good. He was tough but afterwards he'd always buy you a drink after the game. We saw quite a lot of Princess Elizabeth. She would speak to you and go round the patients and talk to them. Lord and Lady Louis, [Mountbatten] they used to come round and carve the turkey on the ward at Christmas.

Gordon Perks b. 1929

> **If there's a do in the village now not everybody turns up.**
> **Terry Tandler b. 1951**

Remember the dance hall days?

We used to go to the dance halls. There was one in Wellington called the Majestic which held a Saturday night dance. When we were 15 to 18 year old kids we'd go down The Majestic every Saturday night and try to look as old as we could so we could get a couple of pints down us. Then you might meet a girl who would let you walk her home. It wasn't so obviously sexual in those days - courting is just the right word to describe it. If you were lucky you'd always end up the next night taking her to the pictures. You'd see rows and rows of your mates there, and those that weren't there were the ones that hadn't "clicked" the night before.

Terry Lowe b. 1943

I met some people from the British Legion. They said "We've got a buffet dance tonight, why don't you come?" I said I didn't dance - well I used to as a teenager - and they said "You'll enjoy the music". I was persuaded to dance and I was hooked. I've been dancing ever since. I love dancing. I loved it from then on and I lost my shyness.

Evelyn Hatton b. 1926

We had the 'Palais de Dance' on the Saturday night in the 1920s at the Music Hall. Every Saturday night we used to go, my brother and I ... cycle in from Betton and we'd pay sixpence to go up on the balcony and sit there, and then you saw a girl downstairs, some farmer's daughter usually ... then you'd go down and pay 1/6 to go on the dance floor. At half time we'd go up to Sidoli's and they had a special machine to make frothy coffee ... in the summer we'd have an icecream.

Edgar Gibbs b. 1908

Edgar's Gibbs's knight errantry misfired one night after the ball was over:

> One Saturday night I'd got the bike and the girls used to cycle in as well... and I took one home to Bicton... it was about 11 o'clock ... we cycled and I'd still got to get back to Betton ... when we got there she was locked out and she said," I've opened the dairy window I've put it on the latch". So I pushed the window up and it was quite high, you see, so I lifted her up on the window and dropped her over. Her father had put a bath of water on the inside and she dropped straight into it.

Edgar Gibbs b. 1908

> When I was a girl the big entertainment in Pontesbury was the socials and dances, especially during the war. We used to sing solos and all that and then we had the dance after. Then during the war there was the Youth Squad and all our new friends, the evacuees. It was a great time. I was thirteen when the war started. There were always dances, there was no bar or anything but there were cups of tea, sandwiches and cakes. The girls would not have gone to the pub - not until they were quite grown up. Tom's sister came to see me when I was in my early fifties and suggested we go into the Plough for a drink and I just couldn't. It's ridiculous isn't it?

Evelyn Hatton b. 1926

> I have a passion for Circle Dancing. It's a wonderful form of dancing. It's not Line Dancing in a Circle, it's completely different but it feeds me spiritually. When I go and I'm feeling very hyper it'll calm me down, and when I'm feeling a bit down it will bring me some happiness. There's a lovely group of people there and we're pretty much of a like mind. Normally you meet someone and say, "Hello my name's so and so what do you do?" There are a lot of people and I've no idea what they do for a living because it's totally unimportant.

Ruth Walmsley b. 1943

Terry Tandler just liked to dance:

> I Morris dance because I like dancing - of all sorts - I like traditional stuff. I used to like dancing on the disco floor when I was a lad. It's funny because I was a bit shy but as soon as the music went on I went out there and I danced like a man possessed and it was great fun. I used to go to Bromyard Folk Festival every year. I'd go up there pitch my tent, go up to the Falcon - I'd have a look in the ceilidh tent and I'd think that looks good - I wish I'd got a partner 'cos I didn't have a girl friend at the time. I've even had a go at line dancing!

He explained further:

> I like something that's got a link to the past. It's good to do some team work it's great when you get it right. I like Mayday morning on top of the Long Mynd - at dawn - it's freezing cold but it's something different. One or two come and watch.

> **Dancing at dawn on the Long Mynd could be perceived as slightly eccentric couldn't it?**

> There's a 101 things that could be perceived as being slightly eccentric - I mean who'd pay £15 to watch an hour and a half of people running around kicking a football? The trouble is these days a lot of people will do something if it's fashionable. Just think if Morris dancing becomes fashionable something clicks on the telly - oh yes off we go - everybody would be doing it. Of course with the Morris it's a thing to be knocked in television ads. These gawky yokels, a bit slow like - I mean I know I am one - but the thing is it's anything but locals. Now there's only me and Jim Logan who are locals. The rest are doctors, accountants, college lecturers and teachers doing Morris dancing.

Terry Tandler b. 1951

John Kirkpatrick enjoys Morris dancing, too but for different reasons:

> I think it's the most relaxing and energising thing I've ever done. There's something about it which opens up channels within you in the same way that repetitive chanting does in meditation or the way praying can do. It's a very spiritual thing. It just puts your body and your mind in a kind of harmony. Because of the physical exertion and the mental effort you transcend your normal physical limitations and it puts you into a slightly disembodied state and that can only be good for you. It's not just that for a moment you forget the worries of the bank balance and the mortgage and all that sort of stuff, I think it really enriches you and transports you to somewhere you can't always reach very easily in the way of life we have now. The reason lots of people attribute ancient origins to Morris dancing...describing it as something that arose in the mists of pagan history and must have been there for thousands of years (and there's no proof of that at all) ... it appeals to a very primitive part of human nature and it addresses things that are very difficult to address in our office-bound, traffic-jammed lives. It's just a very explosive way of becoming different.

John Kirkpatrick b. 1948

Ron Miles loved the cinema but in the 1950s there was no 'surround sound' and some of the other clientele left a little to be desired:

I remember the first talking film I ever saw. It was at the Plaza Cinema at Dale End (in Ironbridge) which was a converted malt house which used to get flooded. It used to back flood up the Lightmoor brook and flood the first four rows. The Lightmoor brook runs underneath the roadway up the main Buildwas road, right in front of Merrythought, the Teddy Bear Factory. We used to call it the doll factory because that's what they made in the old days. I've sat in the cinema and had a rat crawling over my feet. That was in the 1950s.

Ron Miles b. 1929

Evelyn Hatton and her brother used to enjoy the pictures in Shrewsbury:

When my brother and I went to the cinema we'd go in the ninepenny seats, the cheap ones, then when it got dark we'd move a bit further back to the more expensive ones. We never went into the really expensive ones - 2/9s, 3/6s. They were upstairs, the really posh ones.

Evelyn Hatton b. 1926

And Richard Blythe got himself a job as a projectionist:

I went on leaving school (age 13) to Bolton & Paul, Codsall, where they were making the Bolton and Paul Defiant. I was only working in one of the offices where we kept a log of all the various bits and pieces. Then I was head-hunted by the manager of the cinema at Cosford to work as a projectionist. That was an education. I saw 'the Great Dictator' by Charlie Chaplin about fifteen times. But some of the short films were super, and we had one or two of the various Symphony Orchestras. That led me to go in to Wolverhampton on a Sunday to the Civic Hall to listen to various orchestras during the season. The projectionist job made me culturally aware - it made up for a lot of things I hadn't had.

Richard Blythe b. 1926

One of my earliest recollections was seeing motor cars, seeing an aeroplane which still had the wire all over the place and canvas wings. I remember sitting on the street corner in Greenfield and an aeroplane coming over giving joy rides from Astley over Shrewsbury. I remember waiting on the night of the Flower Show for the paper balloon - the hot air balloon which they used to send up to announce the fireworks were about to begin. It was a ritual.

Gordon Riley b. 1922

John and Margaret Oliver had a vested interest in the Attingham Film Society:

The secretary, and really the person who ran it, was Di Moss. Her husband was Hodges & Moss, the Agricultural Chemist - she was a very laid back sort of person. We got on very well together. We went to viewing sessions to choose films. The ethos was being able to see films you wouldn't normally be able to see - films that didn't come to the Empire. This is where I saw all the Eisenstein's, 'Battleship Potemkin', the Jacques Tatti films in the 50s, early 60s. It was held in the dining room at Attingham Park. They used to hold viewing sessions at the National Film Theatre and the French Institute. We went down one weekend and from 9 till 7 there were non-stop films. After two days it's a bit hard work! We saw 'He who Must Die', all sorts of things. The idea was to get a broad spectrum of films because we wanted to get people's interest. These were mainly continental films.

John and Margaret Oliver b. 1929

John's interest in film was a part of his interest in the acting profession:

I first became interested in the theatre because in my young days at school I remember seeing Ibsen's 'Enemy of the People'. There were actors in the audience for the public meeting scene and I thought, "This is dammed exciting!" When I came out of the army I joined the then Shropshire Drama Group with Eric Salmon. I did a bit. Henry V was the first thing we did at the Priory School. George Trevelyan was in it and Christopher Timothy. He was the boy - so I've rubbed shoulders! We took Juno and the Paycock on tour around the county. The next year in Ludlow they did Murder in the Cathedral. John Westbrook was in that and another professional - in the days when professionals would perform with amateurs - and it was done in the Parish Church. I think it was a pretty good performance. I was doing the sound and in those days there weren't tapes and things. You had records and you had to be spot on with putting them on. I remember putting on the church bells fractionally too early. The hum from the last bell was just dying out before the thing started but it was great fun.

John Oliver b. 1929

*Margaret Jones became one of the famous "Welsh Dressers",
a highly regarded part of the backstage crew at the Ludlow
Festival Shakespearean productions:*

I went to Ludlow Festival with my husband and son in 1960. In '62
they wanted a lady in waiting so I thought I'd audition. I failed the
audition and ended up in the wardrobe department, where I stayed
for thirty years. We were volunteers. It was wonderful, they spoke
a different language, the actors... to think they gave us all that pleasure
and they're living out of suitcases and leaving their families. I think they're
tremendous people - wonderful.

Not a job for the faint hearted:

At Ludlow Festival there was a matinee and an evening performance.
We had to be there for 12 o'clock. We got the boiler hot because
some of them like to wash before they went on. You opened the tents
up and got all the clothes ready and made sure they were all ironed
and cleaned and in the right order ... You then had to learn, very
quickly, who was changing where, because they weren't all 'changed'
in the tents. You had to, perhaps, go upstairs, up in a window or in a
balcony. Quite hairy really - you even had to change them under
the stage sometimes. The average change was about two to three
minutes - the last fast change I did was one minute. I was very proud
of myself. It was 'Much Ado', as he came round the stage I was literally
tearing his clothes off and putting his others on - and we made it!

Margaret Jones b. 1926

*Dennis Crowther was the booked artist over the county and
beyond:*

I didn't stop in any of my jobs long - because I could entertain and my
heart was on that. But I didn't want to be a professional either. It was
lovely to go out and walk onto a stage and make people laugh and
enjoy themselves. I sung at a Home Guard party up here, 'Bless This
House' and the expression on my face must have set the place alight
because of the laughter: they were in stitches laughing at me singing
such a lovely song and I thought - "that's it - me face is me fortune"
and I kept it like that! Then I went to Carol Levi's 'Discoveries'.
Hughie Green pinched the idea from him. This was regional at the
Gaumont Theatre in Shrewsbury. I came second. Then I went to
the Dudley Hippodrome where I came joint third and I had people
coming after me wanting to be my manager. It wasn't an act - it was
something easy to do - being normal and natural like - countrified -
from Shropshire. Tell them all about my aunties and uncles and what
I'd seen. Get them going with my melodeon and piano accordion,
concertina and mouth organ. Rural stories. Something to laugh at.

For miles around here I was the entertainer to have - music, poetry and someone to make us laugh. I never looked on it as work. People used to say "Where are you working tonight?" and I'd say "Nowhere. I'm going out entertaining to enjoy myself ... I'm going to a party!" Sometimes I got paid. Sometimes it was for the good of the cause. No script or anything. Just walk on and make people laugh - it was something I was born with.

Dennis Crowther b. 1926

And the television comes a poor second to live entertainment:

I'm a bit fussy about what I watch. I liked the 'Darling Buds of May' and the 'Last of the Summer Wine' and of course above all - 'Dad's Army'. I may be using them as a link with nostalgia.

Margaret Jones b. 1926

I don't have to have a colour telly. I watch very, very little television. People have come here and said, "Where's your telly" - amazed. A lot of houses, their furniture is arranged pointing at the telly. The telly is on all the time even when they have people round the telly is on and conversation goes - or is about what's on the telly. I find it odd to go to somebody's house when the telly's on. I'm just glued to it. It's pretty colours flashing.

Squirrel b. 1951

The television went on at Linley Hall quite religiously at 6 o'clock and would stay on until 10 o'clock when Lady Moore retired to bed.

Lady Moore was very keen on 'tele-suppers' where we all sat in a row in front of the TV set and watched some terrible games show.

Justin Coldwell b. 1953

Edgar Gibbs's father in law won at the Olympic Games!

Tell me about this rather splendid watch.

It's a gold watch which my wife's father won in 1906 at the Much Wenlock Olympian Society. First prize was awarded to RT Jervis for tilting with rings, over hurdles, June 5 1906 ...
It was similar to tent pegging really, but with long pegs, 6 or 8 feet long I think they were. The rings were hanging down and they had to take so many of these as they galloped along and the one that took the most was the winner.

Edgar Gibbs b. 1908

Of course, some sport may appeal to one and not to another, and fox hunting is most definitely not seen as 'good sport' by Margaret Jones:

I'm very much against hunting even though I'm a country girl. I think it's cruel. There's no need. When I was a child I saw a fox being pulled to pieces by the dogs - I won't call them hounds - and that sickened me, to think all the people around, they thought it was great. I was forbidden by my husband to go to the Boxing Day hunt meet in Ludlow, because I'd disrupt the hunt. This would be around fifty years ago. I did disrupt it a couple of times. There's things like aniseed and pepper you can put on the road. It disrupts the smell and doesn't hurt anything. I've done that from 1950 to now, whenever I got the chance. The hunt was livid, furious with me. The first few years they didn't see me do it and they don't now. The chemist does very well in aniseed sales.

I'd like to see hunting stopped. I did tell one huntsmen that if two huntsmen got off their horses and were drenched in the fox's blood and the fox's smell and set off before the hounds, if they like it then I'd agree. You can imagine what their answer was. I don't see the need, it's nature. It's not for us to interfere with it at all. Ideas are changing. I hope the battle will be won. In 1950 I did this alone for a year until several others thought it was a good idea without getting into trouble or hurting anyone - about a dozen of us started this.

Margaret Jones b. 1926

The local JP was used to provide some entertainment for the locals:

Every Easter and Whit the local JP Robert Moore (our grocer) would pay for two or three buses. The children would pile in, five to a seat, and the driver would take us to the country - out to Brockton. We didn't get out. We just went out and came back to Madeley.

Della Bailey b. 1928

There were plenty of childhood games remembered, too:

The games we all played on the concrete playground were 'In and out the windows', 'The big ship sails on the Alley Alley Oh!' and 'I sent a letter to my love and on the way I lost it'. They were mostly singing games, aimed at pairing with partners of the opposite sex, only we didn't have any of the opposite sex to play with. We were strictly segregated. You played 'The big ship sails on the Alley Alley Oh!' by standing in a long line. One put her arm against the wall and you all went under the arch made by the

next two and so on. When you got to the end you joined up with the first - if you hadn't dropped on the ground squealing. You succeeded if you kept the chain in one piece.

Mary Hignett b. 1912

Times don't change that much do they - although Mary Hignett didn't have an Action Man!

On the estate we used to play trekking, we put arrows on the floor and the person who was trying to find you had to follow the arrows. We played football, cricket, hopscotch - I haven't seen that for years - played Action Men fighting, cowboys and Indians ... Kids nowadays don't do that. They seem to grow up so quickly ... 4 or 5 year olds are just running wild. You've got kids of 7 or 8 smoking. I'd never have dreamt of doing that.

Eamon Daly b. 1975

We used to play 'Marleys' - marbles that is - under the streetlights. There wasn't much to do in those days.

Della Bailey b. 1928

Some games are common the world over:

In Japan it's common to play jan-ken. It's a game in which you shape your hand like a piece of paper, or a stone or a pair of scissors. Paper is just the palm of the hand, stone is the fist and scissors is two fingers. And you play it like this. One, two, three! Stone crushes scissors, so you win.

You played that game in Japan in the 1950s?

It's a very traditional game used by Japanese children to decide everything.

I played that as a school boy in Manchester in the 1950s in England.

That's amazing! I believe all Japanese people think it's only played in Japan!

Toshiro Shitara b. 1951

In Jamaica we had a lot of land surrounding our house and children would come and play 'Young Girl in the Ring, Tra-la-la-la-la', things like that - singing games.

Eulin Drummond b. 1936

I played hopscotch and bowling the hoop, sevens - bouncing the ball up on the wall and skipping. On Pontesford Hill you were just like wild things up there, we loved it. Rolling down and sliding.

Evelyn Hatton b. 1926

In Hadnall, a few years earlier, Annie Bebb was playing the same games:

We'd play singing games in the school yard - 'Here we go gathering nuts in May' and 'The Farmer wants a wife'.

Annie Bebb b. 1908

My childhood was based on fresh air - playing games, football, cricket and out in the air as long as one could. Kids could go out then without their parents fearing for them and Monkmoor was a school which fostered cricket and football and the competitive sports which has been jolly useful the rest of my life. My first tennis court was marked in chalk on the road outside the bungalow where we lived.

Gordon Riley b. 1922

Film crews in Shropshire might be a much more regular occurrence nowadays but in 1949 the world stood still in Shropshire when Hollywood and all its trappings arrived:

I wasn't involved in the fun of 'Gone to Earth' in 1949 because I was having my daughter ... but my uncle Toby that had the drapery shop used to see Mary Webb at her home (when he was a little lad) at the Nills. And later he lived on the Nills, nextdoor to Nills cottage. He used to see a lady with dark eyes sitting writing there - she was writing 'Gone to Earth'. My uncle was in the film when he was an old man.

There was a big showing of 'Gone to Earth' for the local people at the Granada. We were all there, very exciting, that was. I worked with a girl called Margaret Corfield, Emily Griffiths's sister. Suddenly on the big screen there was Emily's mum and her uncle and auntie, and to see them at the Granada in the pictures - to see people we knew - actual film stars! It's still a thrill now to see it for me because it's my Pontesford Hill back as it was, the image of Shropshire in 'Gone to Earth' is pretty much how it was.

Evelyn Hatton b. 1926

An eye witness account from Hugo Jones:

I saw Mary Webb. When she lived in Pontesbury they lived first in Rose Cottage - it belonged to a Mr Perry a farmer at Hinton and he wanted to get into the house, so they had to come out. While they were trying to find another house they actually lived in Highfield which was our house - it was empty waiting for an uncle to return from Canada. I well remember my father saying

"You children, don't make a noise round Highfield because there's a writer lives there and it will interfere with her".
Now, Mary Webb loved children, as you probably know, and I do remember her leaning out of the bedroom window and having a little chat. I don't remember what she said. An interesting thing she would see at The Lion was a pet fox. The Simpsons had a pet fox, on a long lead, and I'm sure it gave her the idea for 'Gone to Earth'. Another thing - if you look at the last few pages of the story when the hunting parson comes in, I can tell you that hunting parson was the Reverend Thomas Canon, who lived at Plealey and used to ride to Pontesbury and stable his horse at Manor House. She's bound to have met him or seen him at some time because her description of Tommy Canon is so realistic it hit me immediately. She painted a wonderful word picture of him.

Hugo Jones b. 1910

Evelyn Hatton was determined to have music lessons:

At school I used to play the piano. When I went to visit my cousin Graham, I loved to play the piano and it was decided I should have grandma's piano. It was beautiful, rosewood with yellow flowers painted on the side, and my uncle Neddy said he'd pay for the first quarter's lessons, which was 1/- per lesson, and Auntie Ethel and Uncle Jim Jones paid for the tutor - Smallwood's tutor. So the piano arrived but when we opened it the keys were all yellow. Some were sticking down and some would play. But I thought - that's not going to stop me - I was seven. I went down to a lady in the village for the lessons, but halfway through, she sent me to the shop, so I only had half an hour! So uncle Neddy paid for the first quarter and mum and dad struggled and found 1/- a week for the next two quarters. Then they just couldn't afford any more. So I taught myself to play on that old piano and my mum stood by me and sang the notes that were missing.

As I got on with the piano, I started to play for Sunday School, then for Chapel ... then for the male voice choir where I met Tom - and the ladies Choir. I've never stopped, so I've never lost it. It's been my life really. It's a gift from God.

Evelyn Hatton b. 1926

There was often music and dance in Dennis Crowther's local:

The Golden Lion was like the music hall - people doing different turns to amuse one another. There was a man there - he couldn't sing but he'd make himself go flat then fall forward onto the palms of his hands onto the quarry floor. He was showing us how fit he was. He used to machine gun us with the stool. I'd play the melodeon for people to step. There were one or two step dancers there.

There was this rivalry - each thought he was better than the other. One man used to sing the Titanic. Another used to sing a carol with thirty verses in it. It used to take him an hour and he was drunk before he finished it because he'd have a drink at every verse. Every pub was the same. We used to walk and visit a pub over the common - same there.

Dennis Crowther b. 1926 ⸺

Richard Beaumond was often a member of Dennis Crowther's audience:

Dennis Crowther used to come quite frequently to the village hall - WI Christmas parties and that kind of thing. And he was quite alternative in those days, which is to say slightly risqué. Dennis could tell a smutty story and get away with it, and you would have the kind of hoots of laughter associated with mildly affronted but actually secretly slightly titillated Women's Institute audiences. There'd be a burst of tin whistle, a bit of the melodeon (hinting that he knew a couple of Morris tunes that nobody else knew), stories that you'd heard before but which were all the better in anticipation of the punch-line, and for watching somebody else nearby that hadn't heard it yet. And Dennis would go down very well because at one level to those who hadn't experienced him he was quaint and to others he was the working man telling his stories such as they heard and told in the pub anyway.

Richard Beaumond b. 1948

Brother and sister Muriel Painter and Colin Brown enjoyed sunny summer evenings in the Quarry in Shrewsbury:

There was always a brass band in the Quarry in the evening. All the families would gather there to listen. The slums had been cleared and the people moved to Greenfields, Coton Hill, Monkmoor - and they would meet in the Quarry. They wouldn't see each other from one week to the next these families that had lived next door to each other in the slums. They'd been dispersed. It was a meeting place and a playground for the children as well. It would be packed - like The Flower Show is, and you'd get that every Sunday - in the summer of course, not in the winter. The band would play, and often a Tenor came ... Billy Bucket would come ... I remember he'd sing 'the Gypsy warned me.'

Muriel Painter b. 1925 and Colin Brown b. 1931

And it was the ladies who enjoyed the sound of leather on willow in Shropshire:

> We lost our ladies cricket team unfortunately, we've all got older. The men's cricket team is still going on with the younger men - but I'm sorry about the ladies team. We used to play at Bourneville. we played the men, we played the police. Rachel Heyhoe-Flint came and played with us once - she was great.
>
> **Margaret Jones b. 1926**

> I became and I still am a cricket fan. The first cricket match I ever saw was at Sydney Oval where we wore paper hats to protect us from the sun. It was an ashes match - I don't remember the result because I wasn't very old.
>
> **Jo Havell b. 1943**

> **Now a good day out is walking in the South Shropshire Hills provided we can get there by train - Church Stretton or Ludlow.**
>
> **Jackie Gunton b. 1945**

Shropshire has amongst its celebrities traditional singer Fred Jordan. He explained the beginnings of his lifelong involvement with folk singing:

> I was always fond of singing. My mum was a good singer and I learnt a lots of my songs from my mother and a lot from the travellers. My mother would perhaps get up at a concert to sing but I don't know how I came to perform - just happened to be an easy shilling I think!
>
> **Fred Jordan b. 1922**

Fred's songs have been collected for posterity:

> First time I got involved in singing as a career I was working for the blacksmith, just after the war. There was a chap called Alan Lomax, came over hunting for songs. There was a big concert on in the Festival Hall. I'd never been out of Shropshire before but I went to sing at this concert. We went to London on the train and then seemed to travel all over the place. I didn't mind my first performance at all. I shut my eyes, I think. I sang the 'Banks of the Sweet Primroses' and the 'Farmer's Boy' - I think.
>
> **Fred Jordan b. 1922**

And, of course, there's always the garden:

I like my garden, you've got to have a bit of work, you can't do nothing. My brother was a very keen gardener even when we were at school. I've a good garden although I say it myself but I feed it pretty well, that's the heart of gardening, feeding it. It doesn't matter how good a gardener you are if the soil is poor you won't get the same results. I never use any artificial manure at all, I don't see the necessity for it. I don't think it's good - a lot of these sprays and that must go into the ground. I think if we'd use less people would be a lot healthier.

Fred Jordan b. 1922

I don't like gardening. I Don't mind digging and planting vegetables - but flowers and that seem like punishment.
Richard Blythe b. 1926

I make replica long-face clocks - grandfather clocks - I love fiddling with things - I remember a teacher making me a Stuart Engine ... last Christmas my family bought me a kit for one. Then I went to a clock-making class at Codsall and the Horological Institute at Newark. I love to get out there and fiddle - people bring me their clocks to mend.

Richard Blythe b. 1926

A stroll to Dennis Crowther's relatives was more of a marathon for lesser mortals:

My mother's uncle went for a stroll - all the way from Corley which is by Clee Hill to Bewdley to see his sister. It's about fifteen miles I think. He was walking for hours. When he got there she said "It's our George! Come in and have a cup of tea". And he said "No thank you I had one just before I came out"!

Dennis Crowther b. 1926

With the refurbishment of the Village Halls came the odd problem:

When Aston on Clun opened its new village hall three or four years ago, they bought a rather nice sprung maple second hand floor from somewhere and shoehorned it nicely into the available space. On the opening night the boys at the bar discovered that if they all jumped up and down at the same time the band at the other end fell over as the ripple passed down the floor.

Richard Beaumond b. 1948

The last word from Ivor Southorn about Broseley's riotous past:

My brother and myself had the Bladen Club (which is now the Birchmeadow Centre in Broseley). In the mid sixties on a Sunday morning we'd get people coming in coaches from working men's clubs in the West Midlands for breakfast. Ham and two eggs for about six 50-seater coaches. So you needed a heck of a big frying pan. They'd arrive about half past nine with two small barrels of beer, go off for a ride around Church Stretton and come back again at 12 o'clock. Unbeknownst to the locals, we'd lay on a comedian and a stripper. You'd keep the presence of the stripper a secret because if some local chap sneaked into the show his wife would come on Monday morning crying her eyes out because he'd been looking at another woman stripping off. It was a bit daring for those days. The strippers came from Birmingham or Coventry. I'd act as compere and they'd strip off in front of you - so I used to turn away till I got used to it. But we had one problem once with a stripper who took such a long time to come on I had to go and find her. She said she couldn't go on because her father had come on one the coaches and he didn't know she did it. So we had to arrange for the father to be taken out and bought a drink in the lounge next door and kept there whilst she performed. We had a girl come once in a Jaguar. She was smart - she looked more like a headmistress than a stripper. Once they'd stripped off they'd get a bit enthusiastic. As at the Windmill in London, they weren't supposed to move when they were naked, but it all got a bit lax and they started sitting on fellas' knees.

So there was lap dancing in Broseley in the 1960s?

Yes. But there was no nonsense ... except as closing time approached at 2pm when they'd order three pints to drink in ten minutes, as if someone was going shoot them at five past two. Then they'd be off back to the Black Country.

Ivor Southorn b. 1925

CHAPTER 13

GOING PLACES

Shropshire folk reflect on their first car or their first train ride. There was talk of the difficulty of travelling ten miles and yet some people were happy to hop across the Channel or joined the Navy so they could see far off places. How much have things changed? Is it easier to get from Broseley to Bridgnorth on a Sunday than it was? The rural transport system comes under close scrutiny and the perennial debate of the need for cars.

> **I'd never been to Shrewsbury until I was eleven, and we were only twenty miles away!**
>
> **Edgar Gibbs b. 1908**

Gordon Rose was a little shocked by the facilities in France:

The first time I went abroad was with my school in the 1930s. We were supposed to learn French. We had a very progressive headmaster who was always trying to arrange things to get us going. We went to Paris on the first occasion and I think that did more for me culturally because it was the first time I'd been away from home. I mean the squat loos were a terrific cultural shock. The fact that we only had cold water didn't do a lot to cement my relationship with the French. Montreux was a more enjoyable situation as far as I was concerned, but on both occasions we were dragged off to listen to recitations of poetry in French which after two words you lost the whole trail of the thing. At least I had that experience.

Gordon Rose OBE b.1916

Mary Hignett was ready to battle through the snow to come home to Shropshire:

I used to come home every weekend and I never missed. The bus ran every Friday and Sunday, the driver with his spade in the cab. They really made an effort, more so than they would today. I don't know if it was more vital to get through, we didn't rely so much on things coming in, the town and the area were much more self-sufficient.

In 1947 we saw all the snow we wanted to. First of all the children couldn't get to school; so at first we only had the town children. Then as the Milk Marketing Board lorries cleared the lanes to get to the isolated farms to get the milk (to save it from being thrown down the drains) the children were able to get down to the road and the bus, particularly the ones doing exams. But it was very much do as you felt you could at the time. At the worst I saw snow eight to ten feet deep in places. It went on until the last week in March from the last week in January.

Mary Hignett b. 1912

Gordon Rose heaved a sigh of relief at the advent of the package holiday:

The package holiday came along. We were never great pioneers, they were convenient and I hadn't got a lot of time to research things. The one occasion I arranged a holiday personally, we took the car over to the south of France, it rained pretty nearly the whole three weeks and I got the blame for it. So I said to myself, "I'm not going to do this again". We ended up in a French cinema with the rain absolutely pouring down listening to Henry V - in French of course.

Gordon Rose OBE b. 1916

Train travel seemed to be the best way around the county, too:

As a young girl I went to Shrewsbury from Pontesbury. I went on the train. That's how we went to the pictures on a Saturday as well. I didn't go to town much in the week but people tended to go on the train more than the bus. It was lovely all through the fields, it was a wonderful ride until Dr Beeching closed it with all the others.

Evelyn Hatton b. 1926

Gordon Rose charts his progress up the transport ladder:

My father's first car was a thing called the Stoneleigh which was specially designed for commercial travellers. It had one seat in the front and three seats behind, where he put his samples and so on. Made in Coventry. Of course planning a journey in those days - we went to stay with some friend in Yarmouth and my father had to work out the routes on the maps of all the towns we were going through. I remember it was the most miserable journey because it rained practically all the time and the roof leaked. We ran out of petrol. I think that was its lowest point. Then we got a better car. A Standard. When I went to University we bought a 2-seater Austin 7 which had done about 100 miles for £85 and kept that till after the war. Then when I went from the Queen Elizabeth Hospital in Birmingham to the Orthopaedic Hospital, I suddenly became rich because we were allowed £200 a year to run

a car to go to distant clinics. Then we had an Austin 10.
So yes, we saw the evolution. When I became a consultant
we moved up through various Jaguars and I've now moved
back to a Nissan Micra. It's got everything and it always starts.

Gordon Rose OBE b. 1916

*Marie Kelly wasn't convinced the benefits of the car were
for her:*

My first recollection of being in a car is being taken on a taxi trip
on Victory Day 1919. It was a big celebration for the end of the
First World War and they gave children a ride in a taxi. It was a
terrible day, pouring with rain. I remember being shoved into this
taxi, absolutely terrified. I was on the floor, petrified, and I cried
all the way up to The Column, round The Column and all the
way back. And when I got out I was still crying and my mother
said, "You silly girl, all the other children are enjoying it".

Marie Kelly b. 1914

And Darren Fountain still isn't convinced:

There have to be people in Bridgnorth just use them [cars] to
go into town. There could be some laws, say, if you live within
a mile radius of where you're travelling you do not need a car.

Darren Fountain b. 1987

Part of growing up is leaving the nest. Squirrel started early:

I just couldn't wait to get old enough - to get big enough to start
travelling. When I was four I had a little 3 wheeler bike and I turned
up at my aunt's one day. She said, "Where's you mum?" And I said,
"She's at home" - it was about 3 miles away. What I'd done was
followed the bus route. I never saw my trike again - it was taken
off me. I've never had a problem going places. When I was fourteen
I went to Liverpool for the day - I hitched. I spent the weekend
there and had a great time. Sunday morning on the pier head -
the blokes on the soapbox. There was a preacher all doom and
gloom and I was banging him back with the words - and he couldn't
get past me and I couldn't get any further past him and we were both
talking at the same time. We carried on for about five minutes and
then I thought, "Well I can talk all day and so can he". So I turned
away and there was a lad standing behind me - about my age and
he was laughing his head off. He came over and said, "That was
brilliant" and I went home with him and stayed all day and his
mum fed me. I stayed the night and went home the next day.

Squirrel b. 1951

From Bomere Heath to Shrewsbury:

I used to come into Shrewsbury on a Wednesday on the
Williamson's bus to go to Singletons to buy the cigarettes and
tobacco, then to Morris's to buy the confectionery, and then
on to Nurse Morgan's home where my sister was the cook and
she'd give us a cup of tea and a cream cake. So Shrewsbury was
exciting for me as a lad seeing all the shops selling toys and
clothes. Sometimes we lads would run the five miles into
Shrewsbury bowling a hoop all the way.

Alf Cheadle b. 1922

**Welshpool was a foreign country wasn't it?
And Church Stretton was a Sunday School outing.**

Muriel Painter b. 1925

Bert and I have about three holidays a year, we've been up to
Scotland, Falmouth and the Cotswolds. We go with Owen's,
the Coach from Oswestry. Bert doesn't have to drive and they
always have lovely trips. I've been abroad, I'd like to go again.
I went to the first World War battlefields. When we were at
Pontesbury, Tom, my first husband and I were just happy to be
at home but - I don't know - after Tom died (he was ill for four
years). He died in 1979 and I was only 52 then. It was young,
you know to give up. So after a year or two I went away, to
Germany, to Austria and the Battlefields. I'd not been abroad
before I was 52.

Evelyn Hatton b. 1926

**Telford Centre isn't central to anywhere, it's just stuck
out in the middle of nowhere, only accessible by bus
or car.**

Katherine Soutar b. 1963

*The Government's public transport policy doesn't seem to
have been a resounding success in Shropshire:*

There are some drawbacks to living in Shropshire. The public
transport system is abominable. It's really very hard to get around
if you haven't got your own car. There are times when I miss the
city. I visit my brother who lives in London but I wouldn't want to
live there all the time. For me there are very few drawbacks to
living in Shropshire because I've made my own kind of life here.
It's a good life.

Ruth Walmsley b. 1943

*Some more exotic vistas tempted Maisie Thompson when
she was a young woman:*

My favourite uncle, the Reverend Charles Posnett, was a missionary
in India and instead of going out to France, which was usual for
a girl who could afford it, I went to India. I went out for pleasure,
to be with my uncle, but I helped in the hospital and taught English
in the school to be useful. We lived in my uncle's house, upstairs
to get the breeze. In those days I had a camel to ride ... there being
no roads at all. Awkward beasts they are. They kneel down and
you get on the saddle. You give them a grunt and they get up and
go. There were Tigers, but they didn't bother much with English
people because it was so much easier for them to get a small
Indian boy.

It was there that I met my future husband, Thomas Thompson,
who was working with my uncle. I don't remember falling in love
with him. It was more a kind of drifting together. The only private
place in India was up on the roof and we had long chairs to sit
out there and talk We were married in Medak in 1925 in the new
cathedral which my uncle was responsible for building with my
husband's help. Everybody sat on the floor except for the few
English people who were in pews. I suppose a thousand people
were there. I'd been to Madras - which was our only English
shopping place - to buy a wedding dress. But I hadn't realised
that my sister had made one in England for me and sent it out.
So it was great fun. I had two wedding dresses. I wore the one
that my sister had sent because she'd had a bodice made of
mother's old wedding dress with new material draped over it.
I went up to the hills for my honeymoon to my uncle's holiday
house in a eucalyptus forest. The bearers cut branches and put
them under the bed. So there was always this lovely vague smell
of eucalyptus ... much nicer than the bottled stuff!

Maisie Thompson b. 1896

Jo Havell also went a long way from home:

When I was eight years of age we went to Sydney, Australia.
My father was in an occupation in England which was really very
hard work and low pay, life became very close. We were still in

141

rationing, just after the war. He had a two bedroom rented house which he could see no prospect of improving upon, and he felt that there was a better opportunity to bring up a family of three growing children in Australia ... in fact it was a better life. We had lots of space. He had much better access to different foods and that was very important to him - fresh vegetables and stuff.

Jo Havell b. 1943

Perhaps Mary Stone's coming to Shropshire was going places:

Quite suddenly my husband decided he was going to write the world's best historical novel ... and to do this he was going to retire to nowhere and write it. No-one paid any attention to him, we were in Kent at the time ... we just thought he'd get over that. A midlife crisis, it would go. But he found an advertisement in the Times, advertising a very, very isolated farmhouse in Shropshire at a place called Pentre Hodre between Clun and Knighton - he thought this was where inspiration was really going to take off. And he did it, and I got quite bolshie and said, "You do what you like, I'm not coming ... I'll see you every weekend". That didn't work and we did all move ...

Mary Stone b. 1932

Or we could put a new a new 'spin' on Going Places. The pipes made by the Southorn family in Broseley were world famous:

Southorn's the clay pipe works in Broseley was established in 1823 and by 1890 we employed ninety people. I worked there when I came out of the RAF after the war and one day a reporter and photographer came round from The Sunday Pictorial to take photographs of our show case full of unusual shaped pipes. There was one there made by my father in 1933 that was 18ft 6ins long and shaped like a Catherine wheel with a bowl in the middle and a stem that went round and round. It was smokeable; there was a hole all the way through it. There was another one shaped like a spring about 10 inches high with the bowl at the bottom and the mouthpiece at the top. They took a photograph of one of the girls smoking this clay pipe and it got into "Titbits" magazine. Anyhow, a couple of weeks later we had a letter from the Egyptian Embassy in London saying, "His Royal Highness King Farouk was a collector of unusual items and could he have one of these pipes?" So King Farouk must have been reading "Titbits". We took no notice of this letter because the pipes were difficult to make. So they sent another letter and they eventually found out we'd got one of those sit up and beg telephones and they rang up. We said if we made it, it wouldn't get out there in one piece because the only thing they were packed in was chaff (which had been thrashed from wheat) and you couldn't export chaff in case of foot and mouth disease. So they told us to make it and bring it down to the Egyptian Embassy in London and they'd send it out on his own personal plane. We couldn't resist that. So we made this pipe and packed it in a box to take down to the Egyptian Embassy the next day ... and during the night he got kicked out by General Neguib (who seized power on July 23rd 1952). So we've still got the pipe upstairs.

Ivor Southorn b. 1925 ———

CHAPTER 14

LIFE & DEATH

Stories of near death experiences, opinions on the National Health Service and bananas as a cure for Tuberculosis. Stories about donating blood and nursing in the early part of the century plus an amazing invention to measure how we walk. Shropshire people talk about their attitudes to life and death over the century.

> **I won't say I've been fascinated with death, but I've been interested.**
>
> **Gordon Perks b. 1929**

I started my nursing career during the war. I lied about my age. My family had joined up, my brother and all that, and I wanted to very much. Since the age of nine, I'd always wanted to be a nurse. I started in 1943 as a VAD in the Red Cross. That's a Volunteer Aid Detachment Nurse. We nursed the forces at Ashford Hall (near Ashford Carbonell). From there, whenever there was what they called a "flak" on, we were sent off in the back of those awful army lorries on wooden seats and that smelly tarpaulin down the back. So quite honestly we never knew where we went because there were no signposts and if we asked Sister or Matron we were very firmly put in our places and told to shut up.

Margaret Jones b. 1926

Dad chain smoked and he used to say to us kids, "Don't you ever light-up one of these". He used to light the cigarette in front of us as he was puffing it . He was fanatical about that. It was a habit he couldn't break and he'd done since he was eleven or twelve which was very fashionable in his day of course. I never smoked a cigarette at school. All the other kids were smoking all around me but I was scared to. I was really scared he'd find out. So I never smoked a cigarette till I was 21 - married and gone.

Terry Lowe b. 1943

Gordon Rose's research led to an invention:

I took a special interest in Spina Bifida and because the politicians at that time urgently needed to do something and they knew I had designed a walking apparatus so they descended on me and they gave me money to go on developing it. That's why we had the large ORLA (Orthotic Research and Locomotor Assessment) Centre in Oswestry. We've now two engineers but I started off with one. We began by investigating gait. It happened I'd been interested in gait and had spent two or three months in California with a man called Verne Inman who really started to unravel the way we walk. You'd think we ought to know that by now but it's a very complex very energy efficient system we use. So we had electronic gaits which measure your speed and heart rate and this went into a computer and came out with a factor which indicated the efficiency of your gait. I was very disturbed because that's when one of my colleagues in Bangor introduced computers into the casualty department for appointments and knowledge, and he asked if I would mind if he took a photo of me by the computer. I was slightly flattered. Then he gave a lecture to the Bridgnorth Orthopaedic Association on his system of recording, and he said look even old men can be taught to use the computer!

Gordon Rose OBE b. 1916

If somebody died in the village it was a very sad day. Everybody had their curtains drawn.

Dennis Crowther b. 1926

Beryl Gower had a very lucky escape and it is a tribute to her strength of character that she can now almost see the funny side:

There was a fifty gallon tank of water at the top of the garden. It was an old water tank from the loft. I kept it at the top of the garden in a part you can't see from the porch. I used it for watering my courgette plants which I had on a high compost frame. I sat on the edge of the tank and slid in backwards! I was immersed in this cold, filthy green water - crying for help for 45 minutes - I was completely jammed in it. If I'd been an inch wider either side I couldn't have got in. I could the feel the weight of the water soaking through to my clothes and it got up to my neck. I thought, this isn't funny - all my neighbours must be out. I then closed my eyes - I must have fallen unconscious - and suddenly the next thing - someone is heaving at me trying to get me out of the tank. It was a young woman - she was saying, "Mrs Gower, Mrs Gower - don't close your eyes, don't go to sleep," and I thought whatever's happening she can't get me out. She said, "I've got to go and get help" and I must have blacked out. Apparently she rushed down the side of the house and she saw two schoolboys coming from Meole Brace and she said, "please come and help me there's a lady stuck in a tank of water". When I opened my eyes I was lying on the ground. My husband was indoors - he thought I was upstairs resting - he knew nothing about it. It was the neighbour who heard and if she hadn't gone to the top of the garden to feed her chickens she wouldn't have heard my cries for help and I wouldn't be here today - no question.

Beryl Gower b. 1918

Gordon Perks was able to give a detailed account of his near death experience:

All I could remember about it was walking down this very long corridor beautifully lit but there was nothing else in this corridor - nothing to be frightened of - and I got to the end of it and I was reaching out, stretching to get to the door and I couldn't even touch it, I couldn't open the door - clinically I was dead - and that door was the point of death. It wasn't frightening. If that is dying it's fine. It was peaceful, quiet. There is a saying you go through death's door and I think this was it.

Gordon Perks b. 1929

I well remember when I was a boy if you heard your neighbour was going to have oxygen or was going to have a blood transfusion you knew they were going to die. These were the last rites, as it were. The last despairing attempt. Of course we didn't know much about them in those days. We knew there were four different blood types, whereas now they are innumerable. So my first job as a house surgeon was to get patients' relatives and cross match them directly. There was no blood bank or anything of that kind. Medicine was pretty primitive.

Gordon Rose OBE b. 1916

Dr Keeling-Roberts gives his views on the National Health Service:

The National Heath Service doesn't suit me. I don't think the young doctor today is trained to do the work that I was trained to do. They have such an awful lot of writing to do and patients seem to be numbers. They haven't got the clinical acumen that we were taught to deal with things. Everything is sent to hospital ... when the Health Service first came in we had a domicillary consultation service. You could ring up any consultant of your choice and ask them to come and see your patient.

John Keeling-Roberts b. 1916

Doctors used to be held in very high regard. Patients used to say, "Well, I've now got this scar on my tummy but I've no idea what the operation was. I just left it to the surgeon to get on with it." You don't get that now. But I think I encouraged patient power to some extent. Patients need to know what's wrong with them. They need to be told in simple terms what can be done for them. I used to tell patients as often as I was allowed if they had cancer, and some people found this rather extraordinary in the sixties. I thinking of one particular case which distressed me a lot. It was a young man with cancer of the bowel and his wife said, " I can't remember whether he said he wanted to know or not, so I think you'd better not tell him". Mirrors were taken out of the bedroom so he couldn't see his own condition.

Dr Patrick Anderson b. 1930

An amazing insight into donating blood came from Alan J Gardner:

There are possibly few surviving men and women now from the days when there was no National Blood Transfusion and who did give blood in the years between the two wars. In those years there was no National Health Service as we know it now, nor blood or plasma banks for surgeons and doctors to draw upon. In my area it was the Red Cross Ambulance Service members who first organised themselves to be donors and answer any call from a hospital for life saving blood. They found they could not answer all the calls unaided and they appealed to members of other organisations such as Toc H and the Rover Scout movement for volunteer donors. The local organiser was a Mr Oliver. All donors were first blood grouped, and I, volunteering as a Rover Scout, was blood grouped into "O". I was warned that this was the most common blood group and that I was likely to be called more often than some of my friends who were in other blood groups. If we were at work we would receive a phone call asking us to go at once to the hospital where the donation was required. If we were at home and not on the phone then a policeman would call us out. At the hospital more often than not we would sit in an ante-room and the blood be taken out of our arm into a flask whilst still in a sitting position and then it would be hurriedly rushed to the patient where after a short compatibility test it would be administered, still warm, to the patient. After each donation we received a typewritten report giving the age and sex of the patient, the amount of blood taken from the donor, and a short statement on whether the patient recovered or did not survive. After giving twelve donations one received a medal stating twelve donations had been given. Possibly a bar was added for each twelve given for I remember there was a member of the services who had given as many as forty.

It was when I received that first medal that I went through all the reports I had received. They told me that four of the recipients had died. I had been warned that this often was the case as the transfusions were used as a last resource. But I had also noticed that seven of the recipients had developed jaundice. I phoned Mr Oliver and he agreed it was unusual and I told him that as a child I'd had yellow jaundice. He said he would consult the hospital.

The second world war had just started and I never heard from Mr Oliver again, nor was I ever asked to give blood again.

Alan J Gardner b. 1912

Suicide is not the stigma it used to be:

I've dealt quite a lot with suicides. I never criticise. It's tragic when they have killed themselves. They are brave people to commit suicide. It's hard to understand why they do it. The church these days do not criticise. They have a church service where they didn't before.

Gordon Perks b. 1929

> **A very large amount of teenage suicides are gay and lesbian related.**
>
> **Geoff Hardy b. 1950**

We saved a few lives, where farmers became very depressed about the Foot and Mouth disease - one or two wanted to jump in the farm pool or whatever. You'd stand and talk them round. It was a devastating time; you felt for the farmers. I remember once a field full of cows being taken in as if for the milking and over each compartment for the animals was a name, then, you could hear the gunshot. There was a great sadness over the whole of the area.

Ray Wagg b. 1941

A body may be just an empty shell after death:

My own attitude to death has changed in my lifetime. I feel that once the spirit has gone the body doesn't mean very much. It shakes me to find how many people go willingly to the cemetery. To me that is a waste of time because the person that you care about is not that thing that's lying there. In the city I think death is regarded less personally than in a small community like this. Wouldn't you say so? But I daren't voice my feelings here because it would be sacrilegious. I have great respect for the human body. I think it is nothing short of miraculous. Seeing a baby born. Seeing how all these things in your body go on without you knowing anything about it. But once that thing which is *YOU* has gone, it isn't terribly important.

Meredith Lamont b. 1915

I do believe in Euthanasia. I've made a 'living will' so that if I'm incapable or so bad my son will not have to make a decision. It'll take the weight off his mind and that'll just go through quite normally without any fuss or bother. It just says that if three doctors say there's no hope for me, they can just leave me to die, take out any drips or whatever's happening without any permission from anyone else. Having seen so many people suffer, as a nurse, that's what made me do it and I didn't want my son to go through a decision like that. The living will wasn't around when I was nursing. My son doesn't know about it yet - I haven't got round to telling him - I haven't had the opportunity.

Margaret Jones b. 1926

The treatment was for TB was fresh air:

My education was interrupted because I contracted TB. Sanatoriums were full and I spent twelve months under canvas in my home garden. You had to have fresh air treatment. I spent all my time on this bed of sorts out in the garden, summer and winter. It got very bad at one time and mum put me in the outside washhouse, but other than that I was out in the garden. I'd be about seven and a half or eight.

Ray Wagg b. 1941

There was a lot of talk about VD in the Navy - it was drummed into you. There was one street in Malta called The Gut (Straight Street). The girls were standing outside and you had to take your cap off because if you wore it the girls would snatch it off you, and you'd have to follow them in and pay them to get your cap back even if you didn't want anything else.

Gordon Perks b. 1929

Mourning was a very serious business in the early part of the century:

I don't remember how many years after my father's death it was we had to wear the mourning black, but it seemed like an eternity. Now of course you don't have to wear it. My mother said, "For goodness sake don't come to my funeral all dressed in black - wear colours."

Dorothy Lutner b. 1899

I almost look forward to death. I had very strong conviction I was due to 'go home' when I was ninety-four. I'd got the date fixed. Then something happened. Granddaughter Caitlin was born with cystic fibrosis which greatly upset her mother and her grandmother. They were bereft. They so longed for this baby. I think I had to stay because I was the only person at that time who could help. I was able to change their whole attitude. So I've got to stay on a bit longer now. That day was the most joyous of my life because I so wanted to go home. I wanted to see God. I shall never see Him of course. You can't see Him. But to be more intimate with Him. I was so disappointed.

The Reverend John Ayling b. 1902

Margaret Jones had a very lucky escape:

I had an accident in 1954. My son was very young and there wasn't a Sunday school here [Ashford Carbonell]. We were going to Ludlow to go to Sunday school, we walked down to the Ashford crossroads and we were waiting there for the bus. A car turned into Ashford with no hand signal, another overtook it at speed and hit me to the other side of the road. I pushed my son out of the way - suppose it's instinct - and the whole of my right-hand side was smashed. Since then I've had 22 operations, they put me together and I had to learn to walk again. From then on I decided I was going to learn to live ... so I had a chance to go on television which I did, I started playing cricket and that was the beginning of a new life

Margaret Jones b. 1926

It was fantastic then [when I had TB] how the neighbours were towards my mum and especially towards me. At the time bananas were on ration. The neighbours used to save their ration tokens for my mum and gave them to her and she bought the bananas which were a requirement for my treatment. They were wonderful people, the neighbours in Church Aston.

Ray Wagg b. 1941

I trust that the life that is in me, comes through me and enervates me, held me before life and will hold me afterwards. I haven't got a clue whether I go on as an individual being or whether as part of the ocean, as a wave. In my worst moment death is quite scary. Well this is all I know. As to what happens after, I'll leave that for them. As for now I treasure my aliveness.

Geoff Hardy b. 1950

Battle of Britain pilot, Peter Dawbarn, found bureaucracy was his downfall:

I finished work suffering from depression and I'd been going backwards and forwards to Shelton Hospital to see a consultant psychiatrist there. You see, I think I couldn't adjust to change. I was working at the County Council in education welfare and things were being computerised. I had a job where I was writing an awful lot of letters. People were writing in to me about problems with their children's education and I was writing individual letters back when suddenly I was told, "You don't do that any more. You now have to send standard letters." There was a word processor and I had to send letter 'A' to so and so. I couldn't accept this. I felt I was in a job where I was giving a personal service to people, and suddenly it was all automatic and I just blew my top. It's unfortunate that they call it depression because everybody gets depressed but clinical depression is a completely different thing. It's an illness and you get panic attacks and it's quite different. I wish they'd call it something else. It's an old fashioned nervous breakdown, that's what it is really.

It's interesting that you could survive being a fighter pilot in The Battle of Britain but you couldn't survive a change of work procedures?

Well, when you're in an air battle you're on your own. You make your own decisions. You do what you think is right. Whereas when you're in a big organisation you don't have any control over what's happening to you. It's all down to other people.

Peter Dawbarn b. 1921

To end, a poignant story about the death of a child:

We'd always wanted a boy and Huw was a total accident and a real bonus. But my son was just eight when he had one of these viral infections that children get. We didn't even call the doctor for a day or two. He had a rash and seemed under the weather and headachey and I kept him home from school on the Tuesday. Then he started being bilious so we did contact the doctor and got some medicine, but by Friday evening it was clear he was very ill - he wasn't himself. After the doctor visited on Friday he was admitted to hospital. My husband Murray took the phone call on Saturday morning. We'd left him in hospital. Perhaps I should have stayed. He came back to bed and said, "That was the doctor and Huw's got viral encephalitis." I'd worked with handicapped children so I knew what it meant when I heard the diagnosis. I knew then that his chances were not great. So he went into intensive care on the Saturday and on Sunday night the machines were switched off. This was in 1978.

What did that do to your faith ?

It strengthened my faith because - it was incredible - I was filled
with a kind of ecstasy - I know that seems a strange word - but
I felt borne up for about six weeks. I did weep but I felt supported
and I did find a strength. I found I was reaching out to people
and I had this strong sense that Huw didn't want his life or his
death to be destructive things. Does that sound strange?

And when I heard about a couple of children who had been in
Huw's class who were very upset. I actually visited their homes
and took an item of Huw's to them to comfort them. Murray was
devastated, as was everyone else, but it's very stressful and very
difficult for parents to know how to deal with one another with
the loss of a child. Because grief, as you know, is such an individual
thing. It's not really possible to share it and striving to share it is
hard work. I understood that by the time Murray lost his mother
two years later, and I was more able to do the right things.
It's deepened and broadened me and made me more sensitive
to other people and bold enough to say the right things.

***Has it changed the way you view lesser matters, in that
when something tragic happens to you everything else seems
a lot less important from then on?***

Oh yes! And that doesn't go away either.

Cynthia Rickards b. 1937 ———

CHAPTER 15
BELIEFS AND FEARS

The percentage of people going to church has declined significantly over the century but there is no evidence to show that religious belief has declined in the same way. Shropshire people talked candidly about their beliefs and fears, discussing alternative religions, superstitions and their differing views about the wealth of different ways to worship. Also on the list are the ghosts of Ashford Carbonell, witchcraft in South Shropshire and whether Jesus Christ would visit Wellington.

The Reverend John Ayling was determined to join the clergy from an early age:

> I was always interested in religion. I was determined to be priest. From the time I was six I was absolutely certain I had to be ordained. When I told my father I wanted to be a priest he said, "You're daft. People like us can't be ordained." I remember I used to stand in front of a mirror and put a black sock around my neck (because I thought you had to have that) and preach to myself."
>
> **The Reverend John Ayling b. 1902**

But that certainty seemed to be rare and strict religious upbringing didn't always lead to a confirmed belief in God:

> I don't believe in God. I'm not into religion but I was told I must believe in God. The Nuns on one side - the church on the other side. I was totally inundated with the Roman Catholic Religion. Particularly the Irish side of it. The nuns were all Irish. The school was St Patrick's. How do you believe in believing? I can't believe in believing. Do you believe in God - well yes you do - but has God entered your heart? How do you really believe? Do you have faith - yes but how do you know? All the different religions - if one is right is the other wrong? All these questions.
>
> **Squirrel b. 1951**

> I went to a Roman Catholic Junior School. My mother was Catholic, quite devoutly so ... she filled the house with Blessed Virgin Marys. I was very religious at one point, me and another fellow were suggested as possible candidates for the priesthood. I can remember taking communion and feeling a sense of something, grace or whatever ... I'm an imaginative person.
>
> **Bill Caddick b. 1944**

I went to the church school and the emphasis was very much on church teaching, not necessarily the Bible but the Catechism of the church which we recited every morning. The Commandments of course were law and I suppose you were damned if you broke those commandments. I didn't break them. I didn't want to kill; I knew I shouldn't tell lies; I wasn't sure about coveting - I wasn't sure how you did it - as for adultery, I hadn't go a clue.

Edgar Gibbs b. 1908

Vicky Cowell has deep religious convictions and was baptised as a Seventh Day Adventist in 1973:

I can't wash away my sin, I have to ask Jesus to wash it away for me. I depend on him every day. I say, " I have sinned and I come to you for refuge" like you do in the church. Salvation is a hard thing but you've got to work at it, you've got to work at it every day. It's not you going to do it for yourself, it's God that will do it for you.

Vicky Cowell b. 1931

Although the word 'alternative' didn't figure in the vocabulary at the time the hippie movement opened up different ways of thinking and believing:

I guess the hippie movement did go right in some ways. You can see a lot of liberated thoughts now. But it was fighting against the establishment, so basically it was a small unit against the world. I don't think it's gone away I think it's hidden. I think people got married and settled down, but they'll never forget their experiences in the decisions they make in their everyday life now - or in the way they vote. It was all about opening the mind and finding a better way instead of following the established way, which was all about capitalism and money. Okay, you learn you need economics - yeah, but you've still got the same problems, they haven't gone away.

Squirrel b. 1951

156

*Ruth Walmsley believes there is life after death and gave
an interesting account of her reasoning:*

I just have this feeling about life after death. It's almost not a belief
but it's a kind of knowing that we go on. It's more than faith, it helped
me greatly when my parents died. I don't have any particular wish
to go to seances, but the day after I got married (they'd both died
shortly before), my brother and sister suggested it would be nice
to go to a seance with a medium my father knew ... and we trusted.
I went with my husband and my brother brought his wife, both
of whom were very sceptical. The medium knew nothing about
my husband or our circumstances and he said there was a man
called Ron, talking about 'Daddy' forest'. This shocked my husband
whose father was called Ron and died when he was twelve.
He'd planted a wood at his home and called it 'Daddy's Forest'.

Ruth Walmsley b. 1943

*In the south of the county Mary Stone met up with some
interesting concepts:*

I would walk three miles into Chapel Lawn to change my library
books and the cats would come with me and they (the locals)
thought that was dreadful ... a local farmer's wife came in to see
me. She was having a cup of tea and she said, "Now you'll have
to tell us dear, are you a witch?" And I said, "No I'm a Christian!"

Mary Stone b. 1932

Edgar Gibbs attributes his longevity to a little bit of help:

Why are you still well at ninety?
Luck, and having a little bit of faith in the Almighty. I think he's
been kind to me. I'm not a big religious man but I think religion

has a part to play in our lives. I think it's gone down the Swanee terrific these last years.

Edgar Gibbs b. 1908

Knowledge of the Bible has also become less important over the years:

When I was six I could say the Ten Commandments. I was very surprised when on University Challenge they asked what the Tenth Commandment was and neither of the teams could answer correctly.

Mary Hignett b. 1912

Della Bailey was not allowed to play on a Sunday:

What did you do on Sundays if you couldn't play?

Sit reading the catechism. You went to Sunday school, and you just read your prayer book and you weren't allowed to play cards ... they were play things of the Devil. You had to sit and be a good little girl.

Boring?

Yes, terrible.

Della Bailey b. 1928

People are searching for other pegs on which to hang their beliefs:

I'm slightly drawn towards old religions and the sense of connectedness with the earth and nature. I think we've lost that.

Katherine Soutar b. 1963

Former policeman Richard Blythe felt science perhaps gave the lie to Christianity:

I don't feel there is a God. I've always been a bit suspicious of the formalising of the Church and following men with frocks on but I saw the Hubbell Space station showing us 3 billion light years and I saw no evidence of God ... I think that the precepts of Christianity, if you wish self-discipline for yourself, are excellent. If you wish to have conversations with what's going on inside your head and call it God - fair enough ... but I do love visiting churches and cathedrals and I can honestly say that going into Ely Cathedral I felt a distinct atmosphere, a presence, friendly.

Richard Blythe b. 1926

Former policeman Ray Wagg has different views:

I pray daily. I pray about the youngsters from the Derwen [college for people with disabilities], about situations nationally... I honestly feel

that one can ask the Lord many things. The Lord will decide
whether he answers your prayer but I've never prayed to him -
nor would - that I would win the lottery! But that would be nice.
Many times prayer has been a support and benefit to me -
many times.

Ray Wagg b. 1941

One of the very few Jewish mothers in Shropshire,
Ruth Walmsley explained the difference between the
Jewish race and the Jewish religion:

Very little of being Jewish affects my everyday life. I'm not religious
at all. It's just like someone celebrating Christmas who never goes
to church. I think that the religion can be separated from the racial
point of view. I was born into the Jewish race. I am not a religious
Jew. I wouldn't want to be. It doesn't percolate into my everyday
life at all.

Ruth Walmsley b. 1943

Della Bailey reflects on the strict catholic upbringing she
received:

They were [my mother's family] 'over the top' Catholics.
I was a little girl, five... I used to go to stay with my Granny.
I used to come from Lincoln Hill, Ironbridge to Madeley ...
if you were coming to confession you didn't have a drink of water
because you weren't supposed to have anything to eat before
you had the Host and did confession and you were not allowed
to play on a Sunday and not allowed sweets on a Sunday. My Gran
was so knowledgeable about the Catholic Church - she'd pick
the priest up if he went wrong. My Gran - you couldn't go to see
her if you hadn't been to church and you had to say your catechism
on a Sunday afternoon and when you went to bed at night there
was about an hour and a half of saying your rosary.

Della Bailey b. 1926

The word 'belief' does not necessarily just cover religious
convictions. Margaret Jones talked about the "memories"
she has seen by her home in Ashford Carbonell:

At the top of the lane there is a man dressed as a highwayman
- not on his horse he just stands there. Only a few of us have
seen him. You can walk through him, it's like going through a
cold mist. I've done that. I wasn't afraid.

Margaret Jones b. 1926

159

Fear of an afterlife or a return to this life? As with Margaret Jones, Bill Caddick believes he has seen the actuality and it frightened him:

Some houses - as soon as you walk in there's something wrong and you feel uneasy. Once we were staying up in Consett in this big old house ... and we were four of us crouched by this big old two bar fire trying to keep warm. I looked over the other side of the room and there was a little old lady, sitting there in Victorian dress, a black dress with a lace frill and her hair tied back in a bun and little glasses. It frightened me a lot. I turned to the others and said, "look, look!" and apparently my hair did stand on end.

The only thing I can think of is that there are certain places where people have been very unhappy and places are capable of recording that sort of heightened emotion. It's almost like a tape recording. I don't really think [ghosts] are something that come from beyond the grave. It's more like a recording. It frightens me.

Bill Caddick b. 1944

The Reverend Ann Hadley came to Myddle and effectively worked as a Parish Priest before the Ordination of women was more than a hope for the future. She received a warm welcome and became part of history in the making:

I was thankful for a risk-taking Archdeacon of Salop who's name is George Frost (he's now Archdeacon of Lichfield). I believe you can break rules within reason and he took that risk and it paid off. This was after I was ordained as a deacon in 1987. In 1992 women still hadn't been made priests, indeed the vote hadn't gone through. So one day, while I was still a curate in Stone in Staffordshire, the Archdeacon asked me would I go and "look" at Myddle, in Shropshire. I said I would, though I wasn't thinking through the implications at that time. When I came down the hill into Myddle I felt it was right. So I met the people at a party over at Castle Farm across the road. The Archdeacon phoned back that night to ask the church warden what they thought and she said, "Yes we all want her to come." So he phoned me and I said "Yes, I feel it's right to go".

But wasn't there a slight problem?

Yes, there was one woman who didn't agree with the ordination of women. So next morning I asked if I could meet this woman because she was the only one lady in opposition as far as I knew. She began to explain why she was against the ordination of women and that it shouldn't be, but she said, "Thank you for taking the trouble to come and see me ... so ... that's ok. Yes. Come if you want to". So it was all arranged, but when I came in 1992 I couldn't do the communion service in full. I had to do the words from the Bible (which are nearly the same) and I had to get a priest down the road in Loppington to come and consecrate quite a few wafers to last a month and some wine which we used week by week. Sometimes it got a bit hairy because there wasn't enough wine left and we had to ask him to quickly consecrate some more.

So effectively you were operating as a female parish priest before they were actually allowed?

That's right, yes, with no hope of women at that moment being ordained. It wasn't until 1993 that there began to be any hope. But even then it was very scary because the vote had to obtain two-thirds majority. It did by just two votes on that historic day.

So for the best part of a year you were on tenterhooks?

Absolutely. There was a lot of anxiety whether this vote would go through. If it didn't, what was I going to do? Could I go on existing like this? Should I throw in the towel and join the Methodists? I shall always be thankful to the people of Myddle who just accepted me as a fully fledged Parish Priest well before the vote.

Do you think Myddle realised it was taking such an epoch marking decision?

Oh, yes! They realised they had the first female parish priest here, and it was a first for Myddle. I think it was helped a long way by the (woman) church warden having a daughter who worked in London as an executive for Mars. She had shared with her mother how difficult it was for women executives still in industry. So Ann Duff, the church warden, paved the way. She recognised that this was an historical event. The vote went through on that tremendous day in November 1993 and the first batch of women priests were ordained at Lichfield Cathedral on April 23rd 1994. So it was all legitimate after that. Then in 1996 the Bishop wrote to me and invited me to become a prebendary of Lichfield Cathedral and that was indeed an honour. It was a tremendous day for me, for Myddle, and for the whole of women's ministry. I was the first woman prebendary in Lichfield Diocese. I understand that now I have the freehold of that seat in Lichfield Cathedral - if I don't have shelter over my head one day I can actually go and claim my freehold and sleep in that pew and no-one can turn me out! What security!

Rev. Ann Hadley b. 1933

With the coming of the Millennium and the celebration of the birth of the Christian faith there are many diverging views on how (and what) to celebrate:

I'm not going to celebrate the Millennium the way everybody expects. I'm hoping to be in France, in a very rural area. I'd like to be just walking out at midnight, very quiet, ignoring all the noise and celebration that's going on everywhere else and have a glass of wine when I get home. I think it's just learned behaviour. I'm not a practising Christian ... at the back of my mind is the thought that if you are celebrating, it should be a celebration of that Christian ilk. I'd like to think of it as a pause for thought.

Jo Havell b. 1943

The way they're going at the Millennium is not the right way. Jesus said the end will come after the 2000. We must prepare. There's a lot of things in Matthew 28 that are happening that say when he's coming ... the people are not looking for Jesus to come; they're looking for a new world to start with the Millennium; they're not preparing for the judgement that is coming ... We shouldn't be frightened of Jesus - Jesus never hurt anybody.

Vicky Cowell b. 1931

We're hoping that the church will be a lot, lot stronger after the Millennium. Every church, please God. I've got that feeling it will somehow. It's got so low now that it must bounce back. I've got this feeling that something great is going to happen.

Sister Mary Martha b. 1927

The millennium doesn't really mean anything to me. One has to remember it's a very Christian anniversary and that's a myth. Don't get me wrong, it's a wonderful myth. The idea that there was a man called Jesus of Nazareth who was the son of God who is humanity personified, who goes through all of the struggles we go through. Who is nailed to the tree of life like the rest of us, but literally. It's a great story about humanity and about possibilities. Wonderful. I've no problem with that. The religion is political - it's power management. It's also a place in which some personal development work has been done despite itself, it has helped us to grow and survive and has given us comfort. So I don't deride it totally.

Geoff Hardy b. 1950

I don't make a lot of the millennium. It's another season, another year. I'll stay up on the night ... I see it as the 2000th anniversary of Christ's birth if you're a Christian but if you're not it's just another day.

John and Jackie Gunton b. 1945

Emily Griffiths revealed an interesting superstition from the south of the county:

It was considered unlucky for a woman to go down a mine, or even to go to it. It was so bad that if a man met a woman on his way to the morning shift he'd turn back and wouldn't go to work that day. Also it was always reckoned in the Stiperstones locality to be bad luck for a woman to be seen out and about before 12 noon on New Year's Day. Well, my grandfather was very ill and my grandmother sent a niece to the local pub up at Stiperstones to fetch some brandy for him. This was on New Year's Day. The landlord greeted her like this, "I'd as live seen the Devil than 'e on New Year's Day", and she didn't get the brandy. But the Stiperstones Inn had a smallholding attached and that landlord lost a cow later on in the year. Would you believe it, it was blamed on that girl's visit on New Year's Day.

Emily Griffiths b. 1917

And some personal thoughts on the spirituality of the countryside in Shropshire:

We've always lived on this side of Shrewsbury and Haughmond Hill has always been an area where we've gone walking. Now it's very popular and nicely developed with marked footpaths, which is good because it means the wider community can enjoy it.

But since Haughmond Hill has become more popular hasn't some of the tranquillity gone out of it?

There are still quiet places and if you pick your time it can be very secluded and very refreshing. At one time in my life when I was quite worried and waking very early in the morning, I would take the dog and walk from here up the road and up into the woods and see the young deer. That was quite a special experience and it gave me peace and time to think. I've always been drawn to the countryside, been brought up with it. So I automatically turn to having a good walk for spiritual refreshment. Sorting out my thoughts and thinking about my faith, possibly even praying.

163

So Haughmond Hill and the early morning deer are a kind of meditation?

Yes. Till somebody comes past on a motorbike? Yes!

Cynthia Rickards b. 1937

Perhaps prison may help to give a new perspective:

You find Jesus more in jail because you go to church more in jail, obviously, because you just haven't got the time out there. A lot of the cons here wouldn't even consider going to a church outside, but in jail on a Sunday morning you've got nothing to do but lie in your bed. So to get an hour and a half out of your pad, you'll go to chapel. You just sit and listen to Gay, the preacher here, and you learn. You've got more time to think about what's being said.

Paul Taylor b. 1967

Has it come down to the only thing that people have left is shopping?

Muriel Painter b. 1925

Joyce Brand was a social worker in Shropshire for some years. She explained how her previous disillusionment with the Christian faith happened:

I felt a sense of distaste with formal religion. There were several smallish episodes to do with practising religion which contributed to this.

Can you think of one?

There was one very clear one when my children were quite young. And it crystallises how I felt. I was living in a very rich middle class and beautiful village and every year groups of travelling people moved into the area to do fruit picking. One particular family used to stay right through the winter. They were called Smith, as travelling families often are, and their children went to the primary school. Now, the year I'm thinking of we had a bitter winter and there they were parked on the side of the road, coming up towards Christmas, unbearably cold. Their little girl, Charity, was in the same class as my daughter Jo and I first of all phoned the local Housing Department and said "It seems awful in this weather, that this family has no real warmth. How can they in a caravan?"

And the Housing people were splendid and said they'd give somewhere if they had it, but they hadn't got a single empty property. They suggested I persuade a farmer with empty

accommodation to let the Smith family have it, then they
would guarantee to re-house them as soon as they had a
property. So I thought it would be a good idea to ask the
vicar to announce it in church on Sunday morning. But when
I went to see him the vicar said, "I wouldn't dream of doing
that. That's nothing to do with the practising of religion".
Somehow the irony that we were just coming up to
Christmas and yet he could hold separate the powerful,
endearing Christmas story, and see no connection. I felt,
"Do I really want to be involved with people like this?"
But coming to live in Ludlow, and seeing the goodness
of the people who are members of the church, things have
changed for me. I've heard a much stronger socialist theme
emerge from the church. I can hear in the church things
of real warmth and worth. But I'm not an every-Sunday-
morning woman.

Joyce Brand b. 1934

I've nothing against the church but I'm not religious in that way.
I don't think going to church is anything to go by. I've known
some of the biggest wastrels as is, go to church, it doesn't mean
you're a good living fellow.

Fred Jordan b. 1922

*A last word from Judge Michael Mander about the
practicalities of the survival of our rural churches and
traditional village worship:*

Jancis and I go to church at St Chad's in Shrewsbury every
Sunday. This is a deliberate decision we took over four years
ago because we both have rather strong views about the
viability of rural churches which not everybody would agree
with. But we thought we ought to have the courage of our
convictions and move to a church where there is a great deal
of vitality and life. Sadly, and it's an insuperable problem, there
are far too many churches in the countryside. I once drew a
circle with a compass on a map with our home as the centre
and with a radius of 5 miles... and within that circle, only ten
miles across, there were 25 Church of England churches which
people are desperately struggling to keep open. Within a
distance - which only fifty or sixty years ago would have been
regarded as perfectly natural walking distance - we can go to a
different church every Sunday but one, for six months, then start
the cycle all over again. It's hopeless to think that all of those
churches could possible survive. It's very sad but its hopeless.

165

So which church did you leave to go to St Chad's?

Eaton Constantine, where my wife's father used to be the rector and she was the organist.

It's almost like a suicide note, isn't it?

Yes, it is I'm afraid. It's a decision we took only after very, very long and anxious consideration but we made it and we've stuck with it, and we don't regret it. The problem is the rural church now simply cannot concentrate on anything other than keeping itself going, on raising enough money literally to keep the roof on. And this is being replicated in village after village.

What do you see as the resolution to that problem?

Instead, we suggested efforts should be concentrated on keeping one larger local Minster church where people would go so there could be thriving joyous church life. But people are not enthusiastic to take the idea up. It would have been a huge upheaval ... but I do still conscientiously believe it will have to come.

Is there a problem because their ancestors are in the church yard and yours aren't?

Maybe.

Judge Michael Mander b. 1936

CHAPTER 16

WHAT'S NEXT?

*In the previous chapters Shropshire people have been asked
to describe their thoughts, views and feelings, talk about the
place they live and the changes they have seen. This chapter
deals with the future and how we perceive it. It is with optimism
or pessimism? Is the Millennium itself seen as a spurious date
with no real meaning or will there be a truly Christian celebration.
Do people in Shropshire face the future with hope? What will
happen to the planet? What will happen to humanity?
For those who have seen much of this century - is there any
advice on offer for the future? There were many and varied
opinions and thoughts. Through these we find out how people
in Shropshire will gather together to face the new Millennium.*

Squirrel doesn't see the date as significant:

> The figures - two, zero, zero, zero - it doesn't mean anything's
> happened - you can use it as a bench mark - you can look back
> - you can look forward. I feel sorry for a lot of people who
> really take it to heart ... Midnight, and everything is going to be
> all right beyond that time. A lot of people are going to be very
> disappointed when they wake up the next day after the party
> and it's just like any other day - the rain might be coming down
> and you've got to get through it - yet again.
>
> **Squirrel b. 1951**

> I cannot begin to forecast the future of computers. They are
> developing so fast. In about 1950 I joined a discussion group
> to consider the effect computers might have on the future.
> The computers we then thought about were enormous great
> affairs, taking up considerable room space. We never even
> contemplated anything like we have nowadays. We thought it
> would affect big businesses like banks and put people out of
> work. We thought maybe Universities would have their own
> computer and would let out time on them, but we never
> thought that everybody would have their own computer.
>
> **Alan J Gardner b. 1912**

Ruth Walmsley puts her hope for the future into the news:

> One day a week I work for a newspaper called 'Positive News'.
> I work there because I feel it's such an important thing. It reports
> the good news from all around the world. It goes out all over the

world and has a very large circulation now. It's a little thing I can do - I use my old secretarial skills, word processing and editing - I feel I'm doing a little bit to help. There are lots of positive things happening in the world today but we need to look for them.

Ruth Walmsley b. 1943

> **The word 'change' epitomises the 20th Century ...**
> **I just wonder whether the rate of change can be**
> **sustained ... I think we should just slow up a bit.**
> **Ian Musty b. 1947**

Richard Blythe is cynical but hopes for a 'greener' future

The Millennium doesn't mean anything to me but I expect my daughter and son will be having a celebration at their function room ... I don't envy my grandchildren at all. Not just the political problems but the problems of climate. I just hope that schools have indoctrinated young people so that when they grow up to political influence they are going to be able to say what we have been doing has got to stop. Certainly young children are much greener than we are ... I think greed has prevented sensible action being taken ... things are done because someone is going to make money out of them.

Richard Blythe b. 1926

Ruth Walmsley's hopes are positive:

I think we are very big headed if we think we can actually destroy our planet. The universe is very powerful and we get reminders of that all the time, every time we have a hurricane or something like that where are we? We are powerful enough to destroy ourselves, the nuclear bomb is still there - we know that by damaging the ozone layer and all these things is just the tip of the iceberg. But I think we're generally intelligent and I have hopes that we won't go that far. We've been driven to take these risks (with ourselves) through greed and I think this has come about through business.

Ruth Walmsley b.1943

> **If we push it too far we may find the earth starting**
> **again without us.**
> **Elaine Bruce b. 1938**

I fear for the planet. I mean Chernobyl affecting Wales for instance. That brought it home to me. The fact that the whole world now is very closely interrelated and if in Russia these weapons are allowed to decay, or are even sold, then there are tremendous dangers. What depresses us is it's a mass danger - the world has always been dangerous for people - but what impresses us is the size, the cataclysmic effect of these things.

Gordon Rose OBE b. 1916

Last night's newspaper is tomorrow's cat litter.
Gordon Riley b. 1922

Advice for the future:

My life was affected by what happened in the First World War even though I wasn't born till 1929. It was doubly affected by the Second World War. So I like to think that in the next Millennium we will carry forward the lessons of the current Millennium - that wars serve no purpose at all. I would suggest that no generations have had such lessons taught to them by war as the generations that have lived in this century.

Frank Fuller b. 1929

The younger generation are determined to find life on other worlds:

I think the great dream for my generation is finding out more about things like if there's life on Mars ... I think someday the scientists are going to have a shock and find someone on another planet ... there's got to be - even if it's just ants.

Darren Fountain b.1987

But imagine going to a different planet. Wow! I mean, I'd love just to see the earth from space. It'd be so calm and beautiful. It's always been my childhood ambition to go into space.

Kate Lear b. 1984

But is it just the younger generation?

I'm convinced there are other people out there in space. I think there's definitely another civilisation. I'd like to meet them!

Colin Brown b. 1931

Katherine Soutar believes society is too greedy:

I think people have grown up in the Thatcher era with this need for the next thing, whatever the next thing is, mobile phone, PC, being on the Internet, having a bigger car. They're never going to be fulfilled because there is always going to be another material

169

thing that you need to get hold of. I think there's a lot of children growing up with that attitude and I think a lot of youth crime stems from that.

Katherine Soutar b. 1963

I believe that society is breeding a totally computerised people and that's not right. People should live for what they are, not what they have. A computer is a possession. And a possession should not rule a person's life. But having said that, I do have a play station (which my mother plays on!).

Lorna Griffiths b. 1984

What do you consider to be a good achievement of this century?
Beginning to accept that women might have souls as well as the vote. I think that is perhaps an advance on thinking in humankind!

Elaine Bruce b. 1938

Teenagers haven't got the golden future that I had when I was a teenager. I could get a job and if I didn't like it I could say on Friday evening, "I don't like this, I shan't be in on Monday", and on Monday go and work somewhere else.

Mary Stone b. 1932

There are, of course the practicalities to be considered, too:

To celebrate the Millennium, Lydbury North is probably going to put a toilet in the church.

Richard Beaumond b. 1948

John Kirkpatrick is living in interesting times:

I suspect that the physical climatic changes are going to get more and more noticeable and we're going to have to re-adjust our lives seriously. That's going to rush up towards us with increasing speed and scare the pants of everybody, including me. We all know its coming but we're not doing enough about it. The floods in Shrewsbury, Ironbridge and Bridgnorth - to be flooded two or three times in a few months for the first time like that - I don't know how many people have taken that as a sign of things to come but its obvious that's going to happen more and more frequently. I'm a bit nervous of how governments are going to cope with it all. They're likely to make some awful decisions because its all new for everybody. The only comfort I'd take from what appears to be a rather dismal picture is that I'm sure this has happened countless times in the past on Earth. It could be we've reached this stage before and the cataclysm has been so complete that there's been no sign of it.

That's the Atlantis story isn't it?

Yes. And maybe we'll have to go back to the Stone Age banging rocks together.

Would you mind?

No. In some ways I can't wait. I feel in a way that we've all chosen to be alive at this time. We've all decided to come back and have a life while these things are going on because of the problems its going to present us with which we're going to have to solve. It's quite exciting to see how we'll do that. It won't be easy, or pleasant even, but it's something we'll have to get on with.

But do you think the individual living in a cottage in Mainstone is going to be empowered to contribute to the solution?

We can't all be experts but we can all be open and to the idea that we're going to have to change. To be flexible. I don't feel negative about it. I think it can only do us all good to have to do without some of the material things, to batten down the hatches - probably quite literally - and go back to a more local self-sufficient way of life. It'll make people fall back on the spiritual side of life more because that's going to be all there is to fall back on. It'll be a very tumultuous period of upheaval but, eventually, if there's a process of change that's going to finish in a more settled environment, the only outcome can be that humanity will reach a more advanced state spiritually.

John Kirkpatrick b. 1948

I'm going streaking for the Millennium - well I was until somebody reminded me it was in the middle of winter.

Annie Bebb b. 1905

but the last word is:

For Shropshire, wherever there is innate nature, it's taken a hard battering recently. The influx of the West Midlanders into Telford, that's been quite a big bit for it to swallow, but I think it will swallow it and just go on its way, slowly, patiently, placidly and beautifully. If you look at the history of Shropshire it hasn't changed a great deal - I don't think it will come to any harm. Perhaps it's a trick of geography.

Mary Stone b. 1932

CAST LIST

Dr Patrick Anderson b. Shrewsbury 1930
Rev. John Ayling of Bicton b. Dulwich 1902

Della Bailey b. Madeley 1928
Brian Barrett of Llanymynech b. Llandrinio 1929
Jean Baugh of Shrewsbury b. 1930
Richard Beaumond b. Lydbury North 1948
Annie Bebb b. Hadnall 1905
Ivy Bebb b. Hadnall 1930
Richard Blythe of Leominster b. Lincoln, 1926
Wilson Boardman of Kenley b. Warrington, Cheshire 1955
Polly Bolton of Clee St Margaret b. Leamington Spa 1950
Malcolm Booth of Shrewsbury b. Stalybridge, Cheshire 1924
Alan Bramley b. Hartlepool 1948 Governor, Shrewsbury Prison
Joyce Brand of Ludlow b. London 1934
Colin Brown b. Shrewsbury 1931
Elaine Bruce of Ludlow b. Stockport 1936
Emma Bullock of Linley b. Glasgow 1911
Joyce Bunce of Tenbury Wells b. Brockton 1921
Iris Butler b. St Georges 1919

Bill Caddick of Jackfield b. Herst Hill 1944
Alf Cheadle of Shrewsbury b. Bomere Heath 1922
Justin Coldwell of Linley Hall b. Cape Town, South Africa 1953
Vicky Cowell of Hadley b. Jamaica 1931
Dennis Crowther b. Clee Hill 1926

Eamon Daly inmate, Shrewsbury Prison b. Birmingham, 1975
Peter Dawbarn b. Newport 1921
Eulin Drummond of Hadley b. Jamaica 1936

Darren Fountain of Bridgnorth b. Shrewsbury 1987
Frank Fuller of Market Drayton b. Ipswich, 1929

Alan J Gardner of Telford b. Islington, 1912
Edgar Gibbs b. Shrewsbury 1908
Ivy Gilpin of Leegomery, Telford b. Jamaica 1928
Beryl Gower of Shrewsbury b. Finchley 1918

Emily Griffiths b. Perkins Beach 1917
Lorna Griffiths of Clunton b. Worcestershire 1984
Ernest Griffiths b. Lower Houston, Myddle 1920
Jackie Gunton of Prees b. Kingston on Thames 1945
John Gunton of Prees b. Colchester 1945

Rev. Ann Hadley, Vicar of Myddle b. Worcestershire 1933
Kathleen Hann of Little Dawley b. Wednesbury 1930

Geoff Hardy of Shrewsbury b. Bishops Stortford 1950
Evelyn Hatton of West Felton b. Pontesbury1926
Jo Havell of Broseley b. West Bromwich, 1943
Jonathon Hayward b. Brocton 1951
Mary Hignett b. Oswestry, 1912

Margaret Jones of Ashford Carbonell
  b. Warley Wood, West Midlands 1926
Hugo Jones of Worcester b. Pontesbury 1910
Gareth Jenkins of Shrewsbury b. Llanidloes 1956
Fred Jordan of Aston Munslow b. Ludlow, 1922

Marie Kelly b. Shrewsbury 1914
John Kirkpatrick of Mainstone b. London 1948
John Keeling-Roberts of Wem b. Church Stretton 1916
Margaret Keeling-Roberts of Wem b. Old Colwyn 1919

Meredith Lamont of Broseley b. Indiana, USA 1915
Regimental Sergeant Major Liz Lawrence b. Sweeney Mountain 1955
Kate Lear b. Shrewsbury 1984
David Lloyd b. Ludlow 1935
Terry Lowe of Wellington b. Ketley 1943
Dorothy Lutner b. Market Drayton 1899

Judge Michael Mander of Garmston b. Lougborough 1936
Cath Marshall of Shifnal b. Sutherland, Scotland 1920
Sister Mary Martha of Ellesmere b. Ayr, Scotland 1927
Noaki Midori of Randlay   b. Japan 1965
Ron Miles of Jackfield b. Broseley 1929
Leon Murray of Hadley b. Jamaica 1938
Ian Musty of Shrewsbury b. Bristol 1947

John Oliver b. Shrewsbury 1929
Margaret Oliver of Shrewsbury b. Hodnet 1929

Ray Parker J.P. of Shrewsbury b. Llanfoist 1929
Gordon Perks of Shrewsbury b. Annscroft 1929
Margaret Perks of Shrewsbury b. Pontesbury 1928
Muriel Painter of Shawbury b. Shrewsbury 1925

Michael Raven of Ashley b. Cardiff 1938
Robert Read-Griffiths of Houlston b. Shrewsbury 1955
Miranda Richer of Jackfield b. Oakham, Leicestershire 1982
Cynthia Rickards of Upton Magna b. Bradford, Yorkshire 1937
Gordon Riley b. Shrewsbury 1922
Merrick Roocroft of Hadnall b. Liverpool 1937
Gordon Rose OBE of Shrewsbury b. Coventry 1916
Nellie Rowson b. Crow's Nest 1914
Molly Rowson b. Crow's Nest 1908

Lynn Scott   b. St George's, Telford   1954
Toshiro Shitara of Telford   b. Hatano, Japan 1949
Dave Smart of Clee Hill   b. Blackheath 1958
Vera Smith of Broseley   b. Woodbury Salterton, Devon 1916
Katherine Soutar of Jackfield   b. Manchester 1963
Ivor Southorn   b. Broseley 1925
Squirrel of Broseley   b. Kendal, Westmorland 1951
Don Stokes   b. Ellesmere 1923
Mary Stone of Broseley b. Bristol 1932

Terry Tandler of Ashford Carbonel   b. Mitchell's Fold 1951
Paul Taylor   b. Burton on Trent 1967, an inmate at Shrewsbury Prison
Maisie Thompson of Whitchurch   b. Runcorn 1896
Robert Tomlinson of Bishop's Castle   b. Whixall 1957
Betty Toon of Shrewsbury   b. Leicester 1919

Ray Wagg of Oswestry   b. Church Aston 1941
Ruth Walmsley of Broseley   b. London 1943
Alex Williams of Wem b. Portsmouth 1933

Suzanne Younger of St Martins   b. Chirk 1965

Xiaoying Tseng of Wellington   b. Taiwan 1951

MORE BOOKS ON
SHROPSHIRE LIFE AND PEOPLE
PUBLISHED BY
SHROPSHIRE BOOKS

Blue Ribbon Days
A Tale of Victorian childhood, apprenticeship,
love and marriage in Shropshire
Thomas Edward Lewis **£5.99**

An Oswestry Childhood
Mary Hignett **£5.95**

Shropshire Seasons
Gordon Dickins **£14.99**

For a complete list of Shropshire Books titles contact:

**Shropshire Books
Column House
7 London Road
SHREWSBURY
SY2 6NW**

**Tel: (01743) 255043
Fax: (01743) 255050
e-mail: helen.sample@
shropshire.cc.gov.uk**